Finding New Media Jobs Online

Christina Edwards

GARTH GARDNER COMPANY

GGC publishing

Washington DC, USA · London, UK

Art Director: Nic Banks

Cover Design: Tomoko Miki

Editor: Natarsha Bryant

Publisher: Garth Gardner

Editorial inquiries concerning this book should be e-mailed to: info@ggcinc.com.
Website: www.gogardner.com

Printed in Canada

Library of Congress Cataloging-in-Publication Data

Edwards, Christina.
  Gardner's guide to finding new media jobs online / Christina Edwards.
    p. cm.
  ISBN 1-58965-013-1
  1. Job hunting--Computer network resources. I. Title: Guide to
finding a job online. II. Title.
  HF5382.7.E38 2003
  650.14'0285'4678--dc21
                    2003006814

Table of Contents

5   Introduction

11   Art Job Sites

32   Recruiters

54   General Job Sites

77   International Job Sites

81   An Interview with Michael R. Mizen,
     President and Owner of Mizen & Associates

84   Job Search Strategies

93   An Interview with Chris Strecker, a Multimedia Developer

96   Resume Do's and Don'ts

100   The Regional Online Job Search

102   The New Era of Job-Seeking: Strategies for Finding
      Employment on the Internet

105   45 Ways to Ace Your Interview

113   Get the Right Job the First Time

115   Online Job Applications

118   Finding a Good Employment Agency

120   Mastering the Online Interview

124   Getting the Most Out of a Job Fair

128   5 Things to Take From a Career Fair

130   Sample Thank You Letter

132 Understanding the Want Ads

135 Working with Recruiters

137 Resume Traps

139 Choosing Between Two Job Offers

145 Will a New Job Help You Advance?

147 Why Create a Portfolio?

152 Writing an Artist's Statement

157 An Interview with Michael Klouda,
Internet Design Manager at Toll Brothers, Inc.

161 Checking Your References

163 International Companies

170 An Interview with Gary Quinn,
Technical Manager, University of Teeside in Canada

174 An Interview with Barbara Wolford, General Manager at
Graphic Arts Employment Specialists, Inc.

177 Glossary

189 Professional Organizations

195 Job Search Journal

Introduction

Why Should You Search for a Job Online?

There are many reasons job seekers should use the Internet to find their next job. And the biggest reason is this: That's where all the jobs of today are to be found. Job seekers can also use the Web to find out more about companies and careers. Searching for a job online is something candidates can do in addition to searching locally or going with a recruiter. By putting a resume online, job seekers allow employers to find them while they search for employers.

Advantages of Web Job Searching
· Information is timely and can be updated frequently

· Resources are available at all hours of the day and (mostly) for free

· Information is from all over the country and the world

· Job seekers can publish information about themselves on the Web

· Locating jobs and applying for them online shows prospective employers computer-literacy and Web-saviness.

The Downside of Web Job Searching
· Information on the Web can be old or stagnant

- It can take a long time to find what specific jobs
- Privacy and security issues are associated with submitting a resume on the Web

Here are a few of the listings readers will find in this book:

Employment 911

Established in 1997, Employment911.com is a resource for job seekers, recruiters and employers. Employment911.com was launched with the idea to provide an "All in one" solution for job seekers recruiters and employers. Not only Employment911's job postings are searched but also currently over 3,000,000 jobs in over 300 major career sites are also simultaneously searched. Job seekers even have an option of retrieving their email over the phone. http://www.employment911.com

Vault

Fortune recently called Vault "The best place on the Web to prepare for a job search." Vault offers insider company information, advice, and career management services. Vault's career content includes information on over 3,000 companies and 70 industries. Vault's Electronic WaterCooler is the Internet's first collection of company-specific message boards for employees. Every day, tens of thousands of people visit Vault's expert-moderated message boards to share the latest corporate and career news, network with each other, ask for job advice and learn about trends shaping the workforce.

Vault.com's free resume service allows users to post their resumes and be contacted by potential employers.
http://www.vault.com/

Media Bistro
Mediabistro.com is a job site for job seekers that work to create content in a creative way. That includes editors, writers, television producers, graphic designers, book publishers, people in production, and circulation departments—in industries including magazines, television, radio, newspapers, book publishing, online media, advertising, PR, and graphic design. They provide both on and offline employment opportunities.
http://www.mediabistro.com/

When looking for a job online, job seekers should address some of these questions:

How "current" are the jobs listed at the site?
Many "jobs online" sites promote themselves based on offering a very high number of jobs. Oftentimes, however, some of the listings are quite old. This usually means a couple of things. Either the system doesn't update and remove jobs that are three months old or more, or the site isn't remove the jobs that have been filled. This is one of the reasons that job seekers will want to use several job sites in their job search efforts.

Do job sites "match" people and jobs?

Anyone in the recruitment business will tell job seekers how difficult it is to match people and jobs using software. When a site claims to do this, don't be disappointed if the "hits" it provides are mainly misses. Oftentimes, candidates will do better searching on their own that relying on any "match" service the site may offer.

"Jobs" sites versus "recruitment company" sites

Conventional recruitment companies now promote their services and current vacancies on the Web as well as through conventional methods. Some "jobs" sites simply pick up vacancies that are advertised elsewhere on the net. For local jobs job seekers will usually do better to go straight to the source, whether that is a recruitment company or the employers themselves. Again, it's important to make sure that the listing isn't a few months old before wasting time applying.

Going Further

According to a study by CareerXRoads, "most successful job-search contacts made online in 2001 happened directly at corporate Web sites, not through job boards." Why? It's simple. Organizations don't like to pay the advertising costs of most job boards. Instead, employers will post most of their jobs on their Web site and only pay to advertise their hard-to-fill jobs. The rest of their job openings may be posted to their Web site. Job seekers may think this is a simple concept and that's correct. But it's also the most overlooked strategy for landing a good job. This is just the first of several strategies explained in chapter one of this book.

Resume keywords are one of the latest and greatest things to hit the online job search. Keywords are the nouns and noun phrases used by recruiters and employers searching through applicant databases and Web job sites for resumes for potential candidates. Keywords are a relatively new requirement. This requirement developed when employers and agencies began storing resumes in applicant databases. When the Internet became the main means of looking for a job, keywords became important. Job seekers should definitely keep them in mind when designing your resume and looking for a position online. Readers will learn all about them in the article, "Using Resume Keywords."

Using This Book

As already explained, looking for a job online is somewhat different than looking for a job in the traditional way. The Web presents the job seekers of today with some great new avenues for finding new employment. The Web presents a whole plethora of job-seeking resources. From employment sites, to career advice, to recruiters, to companies that only advertise their jobs online the choices can be a bit overwhelming. Where to start, how will your resume stand out, what's going to get you the job? While looking for a job on the Internet should be a first choice in today's world, it should by no means be the only job-seeking strategy people use. The traditional methods of networking, job boards, classified ads, and targeted job searches should still be part of the overall job-seeking plan. The Internet simply expands the job-seeking resources that are available to candidates today.

To begin with, job seekers can start by going to some of the larger career sites like careerpath.com or flipdog.com or others found in this book. These sites can get job seekers started by offering assistance with developing or honing resume and cover letter writing, finding the best sources for researching companies, strengthening interviewing skills, learning how to network, mastering salary negotiation, as well as perfecting other key career and job-seeking skills.

This book offers readers many strategies for finding a job online. Not only are there listings for career sites, but readers will also find out how to design an artist's portfolio, how to check references, and how to decide between two job offers. This book has been written to offer a little something for all job seekers. There are resources for those just entering the job market as well as those re-entering after a hiatus. This book is a great resource for anyone looking to make their next career move. So go ahead, get hired.

Art Job Sites

Art DEADLINES List

Art Deadlines List is a monthly newsletter (via email or paper) with 600-900 announcements listing art contests & competitions, art scholarships & grants, juried exhibitions, art jobs & internships, call for entries/proposals/papers, writing & photo contests, residencies, design & architecture competitions, auditions, casting calls, fellowships, festivals, funding, and other opportunities for artists, art educators and art students of all ages.
http://www.xensei.com/adl/

ArtJob

ArtJob is a bi-monthly newsletter of job listings in the arts fields, including academic, agencies, artistic performance, conferences, international, internships, presenting and producing organizations, publications, and special features on interest. Sample stings are available, as well as subscription information. ArtJob is the source for professional opportunities and career information in all areas of the arts, including: visual arts, arts non-profits, performing arts, commercial art and design firms, film, public arts agencies, academic arts positions, galleries, internships, fellowships, conferences, commissions and more. ArtJob is a valuable place to find comprehensive, up-to-date national listings of jobs, internships, fellowships and other

employment opportunities in the arts.
http://www.artjob.org/

Testimonials

Hired someone who found us through your site! THANKS!
—A New York cultural consulting firm

[ArtJob is] one of the best Web sites for job, resume and career management information.
—CareerXroads directory to Internet job sites

Creative Exchange

The Creative Exchange will help job seekers locate the top graphic and advertising jobs around. Here you will find everything from graphic designers to photographers to illustrators to full advertising agencies with jobs. All are listed with address information and an explanation of the services they offer. In addition, many members of the Creative Exchange have E-mail addresses and links to their own home pages. Their goal at Power Images is to make the Creative Exchange the premier online location for helping graphic professionals connect with clients. The listings are absolutely free.
http://pwr.com/creative

Showbizjobs.com

Showbizjobs.com features positions in film, television, recording, and attractions. Participating companies in recent postings include: Universal, Paramount Pictures, William Morris Agency, and MGM/UA. Visit this site to find out who's hiring for what in the world of Showbiz. Stored Searches may only be used by Showbizjobs Members. When you sign up for Premium Services, and your resume is in their database, you may choose up to 5 different searches that are saved and can be accessed by you, which is a great time saver.

http://www.showbizjobs.com/

Mandy's International Film and TV Production Directory

On this site, job seekers will find international film and television production Web-based databases of film and television producers, technicians, and facilities. Also find current job vacancies in film and TV production. With detailed, up-to-date information about technicians, facilities, and producers worldwide job seekers will want to check this site often to find current job listings and to make note of the changes in the industry.

http://www.mandy.com/1/filmtvjobs.cfm

Media Bistro

Media Bistro has been around for a long time. This site provides up-to-date job listings for anyone and everyone that works in the media. Media Bistro works for anyone who creates or works with content, or who is a non-creative professional working in a content/creative industry: editors, writers, television producers, graphic designers, production, circulation people in book publishing, magazines, television, radio, newspapers, online media, advertising, PR and graphic design. This site is also filled with articles that discuss the current issues in the media.

http://www.mediabistro.com/

Telecommunications Job Search

Search thousands of telecommunications jobs and post your resume. There are always media and art-related jobs on this site. Search by graphic design, by TV, or by film, and find listings that can't be found anywhere else. Currently contracted by over 500 leading telecommunications companies, TelecomCareers.Net is a complete online employment center. For applicants, it's a high-speed career-networking tool used to gather information and search thousands of job listings.
http://telecomcareers.net/

TV Jobs

On this site, job seekers can display the broadcast talent and work experience they have to broadcast personnel across the country. Job seekers can also search for jobs in the Broadcast Job Bank. This area contains links to stations that have their own online employment pages and telephone numbers for recorded job information. Currently, they have over 375 Job Bank links and 75 Job Line phone numbers in this database. TVJobs has compiled all of these stations and accompanying links onto one convenient page that makes it very easy for you to check out what other stations have online. Free access to this information is available by typing in the station call letters in the "Quick Search" box to your left. As a subscriber to the Job area, you also will be able to access hundreds of jobs that are listed by employers each month, many never appearing in traditional print magazines and many listed no where else on the net.
http://www.tvjobs.com/

TVSpy

On this site, there is a job bank, shoptalk, and links to networks. TVSpy's mission is to be the leading Web site for broadcast professionals by providing job seekers, professionals, and employers with "insider" content, community and business services. With its daily ShopTalk newsletter and its Watercooler, it unites network presidents, station executives, broadcasters, technicians, journalism professors and students in a forum. In 1993, the site was launched and in 1997 a job bank was added and the site's Watercooler was born. Today, the Watercooler is a popular online community for broadcast professionals, with hundreds of messages posted each day. In 2001, TVSpy partnered with Vault, Inc., a site dedicated to careers. http://www.tvspy.com/

ComputerJobs.com

This is an employment Web site for technology professionals interested in jobs in company profiles, career advice/help, and salary information. And for information technology professionals, the company provides its visitors with computer-related job opportunities and career-related content organized into 18 vertical skill sets and 19+ major metropolitan markets. More than 4,000 companies post jobs to ComputerJobs.com including IBM, Microsoft, UPS, The Home Depot, Georgia-Pacific, Coca-Cola Corporation, BellSouth Corporation, Chick-fil-A, E&Y, Deloitte and Touche, Southern Company, Hall Kinion, Comsys, Matrix, Spherion and Ciber. ComputerJobs.com is a privately held Atlanta-based corporation with investments from Internet

Capital Group (NASDAQ: ICGE) and Mellon Ventures.
http://www.carolina.computerjobs.com/

Developers.net

Developers.net, a service of Tapestry.Net, is completely
confidential and free for job seekers. Developers.net
members receive jobs by email matching their personal
expertise and desired job location. Developers.net uses
artificial intelligence to quickly deliver the most qualified
applicants to hiring companies first, and notifies applicants
by email when hiring companies review their resumes.
Developers.net features U.S.-based Information
Technology jobs from companies including Microsoft,
Cabletron/Enterasys, Southwest Airlines, and many others.
Developers.net is a proprietary community of more than
120,000 software, hardware, and systems professionals who
are interested in U.S.-based employment opportunities in a
variety of disciplines, ranging from Software Development to
Network Engineering to Chip Design.
http://www.developers.net

Computerwork.com

"High Tech Jobs for High Tech Professionals," job search Web
site for computer professionals. Owned by Internet
Association Group, Inc. in Jacksonville, Florida,
Computerwork.com was established in 1995 to serve the
needs of both computer professionals seeking employment
and staffing firms and corporations seeking quality IT
candidates. Computerwork.com has never been the largest
job board, but has consistently endeavored to be one of the

best. The tools for job seekers such as Job Tracker, Resume Tracker, and Saved Searches compare favorably with the tools offered by much larger, less focused job boards.
http://www.computerwork.com/

Women in Technology International

Search for technology jobs and information for women in technology. Since 1989, WITI has been instrumental in creating opportunities for women to successfully advance in the workplace. They have worked to help women gain recognition for their achievements as well as support and encourage women with their careers. Programs such as Women in Science and Technology Month, WITI Hall of Fame, CEO Recognition Awards and the Executive Auction provide opportunities for women, men, employees and employers to get involved, get noticed and get connected.
http://www.witi4hire.com/index.phtml

Advertising Age Job Bank

AdAge.com is the Web site of Advertising Age, the 71-year-old flagship magazine of the Ad Age Group, a division of Crain Communications Inc. The Ad Age Group publishes two print magazines, Advertising Age and Creativity; four Web sites, AdAge.com, AdAgeGlobal.com, AdCritic.com and GetCreativity.com; and other electronic news services including the Ad Age Daily Fax, The Ad Age Daily World Wire (e-mail), and the Ad Age E-mail Alert. On this site, job seekers will find plenty of art-related jobs in advertising as well as in print.
http://www.crain.com/classified/adage/index.cfm

3D Graphics Jobs

Jobs in 3D computer graphics and animation posted for the US and other parts of the world. This site serves primarily the CG community at large. At the site, job seekers will find: Jobs by Mail: receive 3DSite Job Offers, Newsgroup Offers, Company page changes, a complete monitoring of jobs on the Web right in your mailbox Jobs by Mail Bulletin Board. Q&A about the Jobs by Mail service.
http://www.3dsite.com/#jobs

ArtCareer.net

Art Career Network offers a complete resource for any visual arts career. Access job opportunity listings, a resume database, career guidance, perspectives from visual arts professionals, and links to other sources of information. At Artcareer Network, they see beyond simply "art jobs" and offer a complete resource for your living, growing career at museums, art galleries, educational institutions, and multi-disciplinary organizations as well as businesses related to visual arts.
http://www.artcareer.net/

Craig's List

Art Job Postings from the List Foundation. Known as "Craigs List" a list of art jobs is provided, many jobs are listed. Craig Newmark observed people on the Net, on the WELL and in Usenet, helping one another out. In early '95, he decided to help out, in a very small way, telling people about cool events around San Francisco like the Anon Salon and Joe's Digital Diner. It spread through word of mouth, and became large

enough to demand the use of a list server, majordomo, which required a name. Here, job seekers will find a whole section devoted to art-related employment.
http://www.craigslist.org/art/

Tjobs.com Artists/Designers

Job listings for artists, desktop publishers, photographers, and Web designers, all listed as telecommuting job opportunities. There are many opportunities listed here that you won't find anywhere else. Tjobs.com offers lots of other opportunities in the visual arts as well as in other areas of the media.
http://www.tjobs.com/jobopps.htm

Art Center

Nearly 10,000 people have registered with them since January 2001 and this site has posted hundreds of jobs at museums, art galleries, educational institutions, and multi-disciplinary organizations as well as other art-related businesses/concerns world-wide. If you want a job, the Art Center can help you at any stage of your career—from entry level to senior management.
http://www.artcareer.net/

Art Squad

At Art Squad, they require: A minimum of two years industry-related work experience; demonstrated abilities in industry standard graphics software; and a Portfolio interview. For more information on what you need, go to the Interview Essentials part of the site. This is a company that

focuses on the "art" industry and the people who maintain it.
http://www.artsquad.com

Artist Resource

This site is an artist resource for the San Francisco Bay area.
Included in the various links is one for job listings. Their
mission is to educate, connect, and promote artists and
writers by creating a supportive community. Artist Resource
posts calendars of shows, events and classes, readings,
interactive forums, competitions, jobs, galleries, portfolios,
hundreds of art links, art supplies, advice and techniques,
and artists' stories. ArtistResource was founded in September,
1997. New information is constantly added. Artist Resource
now averages 33,000 visitors and 150,000 'page hits' per
month.
http://www.artistresource.org/

ArtSource

ArtSource provides job listings for digital media. ArtSource is
a digital media staffing agency that matches talent and clients
for short and long-term assignments, contract and direct hire
positions, with no fee to the talent. The offices are located
along the West Coast in Seattle/Bellevue, Portland and San
Francisco/Palo Alto. For job opportunities, search the listings
in the job search section. For more detailed information
about how to become ArtSource talent, please refer to the
section called "how we work."
http://www.artsource.com

Artist Search Agency

Artist Search Agency, Inc. represents creative talent for freelance, part-time and full-time positions who are available to work for in-house or out of their own studio. Interested in being represented by Artist Search Agency, Inc.? If so they'd like to hear from you. Just fill out the form on the site and they'll contact you, or fax your resume to (310) 265-4411. Resumes in Microsoft Word format can be emailed to arsearch@gte.net, DO NOT send resumes that are not in Microsoft Word files.
http://www.artistsearchagency.com/main.html

ArtsWire Current

Celebrating its 31st anniversary, New York Foundation for the Arts (NYFA) gives more money and support to arts organizations and artists of all disciplines than any other comparable organization in the country: nearly $10 million in grants and services annually. Its Fellowships of $7,000 each go to as many as 170 New York State artists every year from a field of 16 disciplines, covering the visual, performing, and literary arts. NYFA also gives grants and services to strengthen small arts organizations and provides artists with career development support through workshops, hotlines, and print and electronic publications. Find many job listings on this site.
http://www.artswire.org/current/jobs.html

Creative Hot List

Creative Hotlist is a customizable online application for connecting talent, companies, and services. Creative Hotlist

has a search engine and enables users to find individuals, companies, and resources for any aspect of the creative marketplace including job openings, creative services, artists, designers, programmers, printers, service bureaus, schools, and clubs. Creative Hotlist provides features for both individuals and firms. Individuals can post resumes, job-wanted listings, and online portfolios. Sorted results can be saved, filed, and accessed anytime.
http://www.creativehotlist.com/index.asp

Computerwork.com

Owned by Internet Association Group, Inc. in Jacksonville, Florida, Computerwork.com was established in 1995 to serve the needs of both computer professionals seeking employment and staffing firms and corporations seeking quality IT candidates. Computerwork.com has never been the largest job board, but has endeavored to be one of the best. The tools for job seekers such as Job Tracker, Resume Tracker, and Saved Searches compare with the tools offered by much larger, less focused job boards.
http://www.computerwork.com

Creative Group

The Creative Group specializes in matching advertising and marketing talent with leading companies on a project basis. The site boasts a large network of client companies. This agency is known in the industry by many top-notch companies. If you want exciting work, check out their immediate job openings.
http://www.creativegroup.com

Communication Arts

Founded in 1959, Communication Arts is a trade journal for visual communications and was the first major design publication to launch a Web presence in 1995. Part of the initial launch was a career section that included listings of jobs available and wanted. This section quickly became a premiere career resource for the professional creative marketplace. Communication Arts maintains an excellent job resource site. Search options have been expanded to include search by geographic region.
http://www.creativehotlist.com/

Creative Assets

Creative Assets is a creative placement agency focused solely on placing design, advertising, marketing and public relations talent into freelance, contract, and direct-hire positions. Find new media, design, and illustrative job listings for Seattle, Portland, San Francisco and Los Angeles.
http://www.creativeassets.com/

Creative Central

The jobs in this database relate to the creative industries. By focusing in on creative careers they are able to provide a site that is tailored to this community of working individuals. There are job listings for new media, graphics, photography, and other areas.
http://www.creativecentral.com

FindCreative.com

FindCreative.com is a job search and job posting Web site designed for the creative community. Additional information and forum relating to the creative job search is available. Findcreative.com is designed exclusively to network creative talents. Findcreative.com hopes to become the premier one stop clearinghouse for those seeking creative jobs and for employers seeking creative talents.
http://www.findcreative.com/

Graphic Arts Employment Specialists

A professional, nationwide recruiting and placement operation providing the printing, publishing, and graphic arts industries with management, editorial, and production personnel. This site includes job listings for computer animation. Graphic Arts Employment Specialists, Inc. is a professional, nationwide recruiting and placement operation. All of the positions relate to print and print production, from pre-press to post production.
http://www.gaes.com

MacTalent

Various positions, including are art-related jobs requiring Macintosh experience. Temp agencies, jobshops, and job placement firms provide a valuable service and can be found here. MacTalent lets you advertise yourself directly to employers. There are no agency or placement fees to be paid. Job seekers may even be able to negotiate a higher rate/salary.
http://www.mactalent.com

Multimedia Recruiting Connection

On this site, job listings range from intranet/Internet developers to instructional technologists designers to multimedia content production. Instructional Designers, WBT Specialists, ISD Professionals and Online Training Specialists represent the type of e-learning talent this company locates for their corporate clients. The types of positions they fill include: Senior Level Management Positions; Chief Knowledge Officer (CKO); Chief Learning Officer (CLO); Chief e-learning Officer; Director of Intellectual Assets Mgr. of Performance Improvement Corporate Training Mgr; Instructional Designers; WBT / MBT, Distance Learning, Simulations, Virtual Reality; ERP Training Support for; SAP, PeopleSoft, Siebel, Baan, J.D.Edwards, Oracle.

http://www.mmrc.com/

Print Jobs

Presented by Newhouse Associates, recruiting specialists for the printing and graphic arts industries. This company's clients are Fortune 500 companies as well as some small printing and graphic arts organizations in the USA. Since 1985 Newhouse Associates has been assisting printing and graphic arts professionals in finding positions. There are no fees to individuals to register with them. The clients, upon the candidate securing a position with them through Newhouse Associates, pay all fees.

http://www.printjobs.com/

PrintLink

PrintLink is a Graphic Arts Professional Staffing Service for senior/middle print management and all digital prepress positions. With offices in the US and Canada, PrintLink serves a regional, national, and international market. PrintLink provides permanent placement opportunities for senior/middle print management, digital prepress, IT, and other key positions in the US and Canada.
http://printlink.com/

Silicon Alley Job Board

New York New Media Association with job listings from design to technical and administrative, most in the New York City area. NYNMA is a popular online destination for employers, recruiters, and professionals seeking employment in new media. NYNMA's Job Board offers an array of new media job openings in the tri-state area. Job seekers can post resumes, hiring managers can post positions, and free agents can advertise their services. NYNMA's Career Development section provides the new media community with programs and services for career advancement.
http://www.nynma.org/jobs.cfm

Coolgamejobs.com

Coolgamejobs.com is a recruiter that tries to offer personal service in a technical world. Unlike other recruiters, they use a technical summary. It is similar to a resume; the difference is that staff members as opposed to a resume written by the applicant write it. Joe Brzoska is the CEO of the firm. He has been a leader in the search industry for video games since the

days when the Z80 was the cutting edge chip.
http://coolgamejobs.com/

Gamejobs

GameJobs lets job seekers quickly check jobs that have already been posted within the system and may be of interest. In the Quick Job Search button located at the top of the left hand navigation bar, simply type in a position, department, company name or part of the country to see what positions are currently available. GameJobs allows you, the Job Seeker, to create your personal account. The service is completely free-of-charge and lets you take advantage of the following benefits: Create, edit, and store your resume online; apply for positions instantly once you have registered; receive email whenever a job in which you might be interested is posted. http://www.gamejobs.com/

Gamequest

Gamequest offers jobs in video games and has relationships with all of the major players in the industry. GAMEQUEST, founded in 1998, is a recruiting agency for the placement of computer game professionals. Owner, Carol Hecht, brings 5 years of recruiting experience specializing in video games. GAMEQUEST focuses on nationwide opportunities, strong client/candidate relationships, and professional career management.
http://gamequest.org/html/page1_html.html

Testimonials

"Carol Hecht works harder than any other recruiter that I've ever dealt with. She got me the job I wanted with the salary I wanted. The

fact that she has such a great rapport with her clients as well as the companies she deals with really helps. When you call Carol she does her absolute best to get you hired as quickly as possible. It's her passion that makes all the difference."

—Chris, Art Director

VisualNation

VisualNation is a collection of information for anyone working in any of the visual fields. The company believes in the process of gathering information from experts and presenting it to an audience in a clear, easily understandable form. Technical communicators gather knowledge from these experts by conducting interviews and reading previously published material. The technical communicator then studies the audience and determines the best way to present the information. Should it be a Web site? A book? A brochure? An illustration? A chart? The technical communicator reshapes the information so that the audience can have access to it and understand it. It is with these goals in mind that they provide job listings for people who work in this medium.
http://www.visualnation.com/
VN1art_job.html#anchor3491922

B-Roll

Here, job seekers will find job listings for news video/ photography. B-Roll supplies information, tips, and discussions on Photography, News, and the entire Television Medium. This site has been developed and maintained by, Kevin Johnson, a 29-year-old, Television News Photographer, or "photog," at WVEC-TV 13 (ABC) in Norfolk, Virginia.

The aim of this site is to provide job listings and information geared toward professionals looking or working in television newsrooms.

http://www.b-roll.net/jobs/main.html

ArtsEdge

Art institutional and education job postings can be found here. The mission of ARTSEDGE has always been to help artists, teachers, and students gain access to and/or share information, resources, and ideas that support the arts as a core subject area in the K-12 curriculum. ARTSEDGE has received many awards, notices, and accolades since its launch in 1991.

http://artsedge.kennedy-center.org/artsedge.html

Artisan Online

Artisan Online brings together your skills with Web, print, multimedia, and technical opportunities for freelance and full-time jobs, not to mention off-site projects. Job listings include Web development, multimedia, graphic design, art direction, illustration, and photography in the Chicago area.

http://www.artisan-inc.com/

Find Net Work

A new media placement agency specializing in senior-level new media opportunities with placement opportunities in Web development, project management, programming, Internet and intranet design, marketing, new business development, and technology management. The company's site also has tips on resumes, interviews, and more. A recent

poll uncovered that more than 90% of all job failures have been traced to mistakes in the selection process and they aim to change that.
http://www.saeges.com

TempArt

TempArt is a Temporary Employment Agency for Ad Agencies, Graphic Design Firms, and Corporate Art Departments. TempArt Staffing has been a source for staffing professional creative talent for over 17 years. Ad Agencies, Design Firms, Corporate Marketing, and Web Departments have listings here.
http://www.tempart.com/

Art Links Staffing

Art Links Staffing provides recruiting and temporary assistance for advertising, graphics, multimedia, and publishing. Their clients are businesses from Los Angeles to Vancouver, with primary concentration in the San Francisco Bay Area, where their home office is located. Marti Stites, a Certified Personnel Consultant, began ArtLinks in 1994 and continues as its working owner. She contributes 15 years of experience from Walnut Creek's Visual Arts Exhibition Program combined with prior work in human resources.
http://www.artlinks-staffing.com/

ArtSchools.com

A useful resource providing Internet references for a career in art, this company's mission is to help prospective graduate, undergraduate, and recreational art students quickly access

art schools, colleges, workshops, and programs based on their own unique criteria. Additionally, artschools.com strives to give students a path from their idea of getting an art education to their career in art if they choose to go that far with it. This site has a few good job listings, but you can't beat the art resources.
http://www.artschools.com/careers-jobs

Techies

The techies.com site is considered "a leading intersection on the Internet for IT (information technology) workers and employers." Techies.com's strong member community—and their data—have become a valuable resource for major media organizations such as CNN, ABCnews.com, USA Today and others in the US, Canada and Great Britain. There are many job resources here, including lots of jobs in the industry.
http://www.techies.com

Testimonial

"I thought the site was easy to navigate, and easy to use for both posting and candidate searches… I especially like the fact that a customer service rep emailed me with suggestions on how to better target candidates with one of my postings."

—Client comment.

Recruiters

Coroflot

Coroloft is a recruiter serving the art industry. With their portfolio services, you can add as much or as little as you want: post a brief summary of your skills and experience, your full resume, or up to 5 images of your work. The Web-based forms allow you to cut and paste directly from your resume. Post portfolio images online straight from your hard-drive. In fact, if you have your text and images prepared you can get build a Coroflot portfolio in 15 minutes! Get new job postings delivered to you via e-mail automatically. When you put your portfolio online at Coroflot you are automatically included in the Skill Filter database. Employers use Skill Filter to match their job requirements to the skill-sets of designers.
http://www.coroflot.com/

Filcro Media Staffing

Filcro Media Staffing is an executive search firm devoted to Broadcasting & Multimedia Executive Search. Network, Affiliate, MSO, Corporate, and Independent Media & Entertainment entities are a few of the types of organizations that are supported by them. Founded and based in New York City in 1985, Filcro Media Staffing provides recruitment services to radio, TV & cable broadcasters, multinational media & entertainment conglomerates, and major corporations developing or initiating their own internal

media resources.
http://www.filcro.com/page2.html

Jola Recruitment

Jola Recruitment tries to connect the best available talent with the best available career opportunities. This is a recruiter that specializes in placing creative people in creative positions. The clients they serve include many top-notch media companies. Every year, Jola Recruitment screens and places hundreds of candidates who meet and exceed the highest standards set by industry professionals.
http://www.jolasearch.com/index_2.html

Roz Goldfarb Associates

The RGA-joblink contains specific information about each of the areas they cover. RGA's clients include a broad spectrum of corporations, graphic design firms (including packaging, corporate identity firms, corporate literature, promotional design, annual reports), industrial design firms, advertising agencies, sales promotion and direct marketing agencies, marketing communications firms, publishing companies, media companies, retail and licensing firms, multimedia production and publishing companies, and online publications and services.
http://www.rga-joblink.com/docs/register.form.html

Temp Art

"Creative thinking is a process in which ideas are born through intuition, developed through perception and implemented through reasoning." TempArt is a temporary and full-time staffing agency dedicated to providing Ad Agencies, Graphic Design Firms, and Corporate Art Departments with qualified designers, Web developers, desktop publishers, illustrators, and art directors since 1985. Check them out for some of the less-advertised positions. http://www.tempart.com/home_frame.html

Update Graphics

Update Graphics features both on and off-site placement, with two offices in New York City and Newark, New Jersey with 24-hour availability. Who are they looking for? Print: Designers, Art Directors, Creative Directors, Corporate ID/ Brand Consultants New Media: Designers, Producers, Coders, Action Scripters, CD-ROM Developers Traditional: Marker Comp Artists, Mechanical Artists Presentation Specialists Production: Studio Managers, Production Artists, Typesetters Copy: Proofreaders, Copywriters, Editors Account Management: Account Coordinators, Account Executives, Account Supervisors, Account Directors. http://www.updategraphics.com/

Visuals

"Visuals" is one of San Francisco's digital arts and Web talent contract and full-time placement resource. This company has been in business since 1990. Visuals thrive in the areas of digital print, interactive, and Web design and development. And they always welcome the addition of valuable and flexible candidates to their talent pool. Their clients include some of the Bay Area's industries like Web, advertising,

design, and Fortune 1000 firms.
http://www.visuals.com/

StepStone

With over 3,000,000 user sessions every month, StepStone attracts serious candidates looking for jobs. The average StepStone user spends approximately 10 minutes on their site per visit, viewing around 15 pages. Jobs that offer scope for personal development and opportunities to learn are job seekers' highest priority, and holiday entitlement and wider benefits packages are amongst the lowest. Check out Step Stone for plenty of listings in the arts.
http://www.stepstone.com

HireMinds

HireMinds specializes in disciplines including Biotech/Scientific, High-tech, and Creative/Media. This company is primarily a permanent placement firm working on full-time roles in these specialty disciplines. They have placed hundreds of job seekers into the area's best jobs.
http://www.hireminds.net

Career Connector

Career Connector provides residents of the Chicagoland area with career news, resume assistance, and tips to help job seekers find the ideal job. Follow the links to learn more about the tools job seekers need in the job search and tips to help you manage your career. Most of the listings are for the Chicago area, but there are a few in other areas. Find creative

opportunities here and consider the move to the Midwest.
http://www.careerconnector.com

The Job Dr.

The Job Dr. is a technical recruiting firm dedicated to helping computer professionals in furthering their careers and job skills. This firm has vast resources for locating the position that best suits your skills and qualifications. Check out the Top Jobs database for a huge list of today's best career opportunities.
http://www.jobdr.com

MBA Management

MBA Management is a recruiting firm that places people in many creative positions nationwide. This company focuses on finding job seekers the exact opportunity they have been seeking with the needs of creative companies everywhere. If you want personal service and help with your job search, you will find it here.
http://www.mbamgmt.com

Profiles

For marketing, creative, advertising, public relations, and sales, Profiles is a well-known recruiter. If you are seeking job opportunities in the area of arts or entertainment, Profiles can help you. Let them find you a unique position in the field. Profiles is headquartered in Baltimore, MD with recruitment offices in downtown Baltimore and Washington, DC.
http://www.profilesplacement.com

Accenture

Accenture is a management and technology services organization. Through its network of businesses approach—in which the company enhances its consulting and outsourcing expertise through alliances, affiliated companies and other capabilities—Accenture delivers innovations that help job seekers across all industries, including the arts. At Accenture you can join ranks with more than 75,000 other highly talented professionals in 47 countries. http://www.careers3.accenture.com/

Aquent

Aquent is a talent agency for Creative, Web, and Tech professionals, with offices in more than 50 cities and 10 countries. Aquent is the Official Talent Agency of the AIGA, and the Official Career Partner of Lynda.com. Aquent maintains a large listing of job openings on their Job Search page, and accepts online Resume Submissions. http://www.aquent.com/

Workaholics4Hire

Workaholics4Hire.com is a recruiter offering positions in many different industries. The teams consist of over 16,000 talented members holding positions in Web development, programming, technical writing, business writing, graphics design, desktop publishing, transcription, translation, clerical, project management, marketing, and many more. They also offer a free searchable database that offers hundreds of current telecommuting jobs. http://www.Workaholics4Hire.com/

Testimonials

"I wanted to let you guys know that after months of trying to get a legit. job working at home, I finally found one on your site!!! Thank you so much I'm telling everyone I know who is job seeking to visit your site."

—*Elizabeth DiGregorio, job seeker.*

"I just wanted to let everyone know that I have a contract with the monitoring company!!! They have been great to work with and very helpful in getting me started."

— *K. Drake, job seeker.*

Interactive Selection

Interactive Selection is an executive search and recruitment company working only in computer games and interactive entertainment. Established in 1996, and with the most experienced consultants in the industry, they operate across the UK, Europe and USA with offices in London, Leicester and Northampton in the UK and associate offices in Los Angeles, USA, and Sydney, Australia. This company is dedicated to placing people with over 600 client companies that include Microsoft, Sony, Sega, Electronic Arts, Infogrames, Virgin, Eidos, Hutchison, and Orange. http://www.interactiveselection.com/

Paladin Staffing Services

Paladin provides interim and full-time staffing, outsourcing, and consulting solutions to their candidate base which is comprised of marketing, advertising, communications, and creative professionals, and to their client base that consists of Fortune 1000 companies, professional service organizations,

advertising agencies and design firms of all sizes.
http://www.paladinstaff.com/

Virtual Search

Those at VIRTUAL SEARCH are multimedia industry
professionals who place candidates in many positions across
the multimedia board. This company can do the legwork of
your job search, and allow you to focus on honing your skills.
http://www.vsearch.com/index.htm

Testimonial

*"I have worked with many recruiters and recruiting firms over the
years, and Marc Mencher is a rare breed. His dedication and attention to detail were invaluable to me at a time when I was struggling
to find the right fit on my own. Marc is, simply, the best. Rest assured,
should I need a recruiter again, his will be the first (and only) number
I call."*

—Development Director, Electronic Arts.

Volt

Volt has come a long way since founders William and Jerome
Shaw opened the first office in the kitchen of their parents'
apartment with an initial capital investment of $13.00. This
recruiter has been placing creative individuals in creative
positions for a long time and don't plan to stop anytime
soon.
http://www.volt.com/

Art Squad

At Art Squad, they require: A minimum of two years
industry-related work experience; demonstrated abilities in

industry standard graphics software; and a Portfolio interview. For more information on what you need, go to the Interview Essentials part of the site. They offer many positions in the arts to qualified individuals.
http://www.artsquad.com

ArtSource

ArtSource provides job listings for digital media. ArtSource is a digital media- staffing agency that matches talent and clients for short and long-term assignments, contract and direct hire positions, with no fee to the talent. The offices are located along the West Coast in Seattle/Bellevue, Portland and San Francisco/Palo Alto. For job opportunities, search the listings in the job search section. For more detailed information about how to become ArtSource talent, please refer to the section called "how we work."
http://www.artsource.com

Artist Search Agency

Artist Search Agency, Inc. represents creative talent for freelance, part-time, and full-time positions who are available to work for in-house or out of their own studio. Interested in being represented by Artist Search Agency, Inc.? If so they'd like to hear from you. Just fill out the form on the site and they'll contact you, or fax or email your resume to them.
http://www.artistsearchagency.com/main.html

Creative Group

The Creative Group specializes in matching advertising and marketing talent with companies on a per-project basis. This

group has a large group of clients that offer full-time, part-time, and contract employment. They have many immediate openings on all different levels of expertise.
http://www.creativegroup.com

Creative Assets

Creative Assets is a creative placement agency focused solely on placing design, advertising, marketing and public relations talent into freelance, contract, and direct-hire positions. This recruiter serves many job applicants in the creative arts. Find new media, design, and illustrative job listings for Seattle, Portland, San Francisco, and Los Angeles.
http://www.creativeassets.com/

Multimedia Recruiting Connection

On this site, job listings range from Intranet/Internet developers to instructional technologists designers to multimedia content production. Instructional Designers, WBT Specialists, ISD Professionals and Online Training Specialists represent the type of e-learning talent this company locates for their corporate clients. The types of positions they fill include: Senior Level Management Positions; Chief Knowledge Officer (CKO); Chief Learning Officer (CLO); Chief e-learning Officer; Director of Intellectual Assets Mgr. of Performance Improvement Corporate Training Mgr; Instructional Designers; WBT / MBT, Distance Learning, Simulations, Virtual Reality; ERP Training Support for; SAP, PeopleSoft, Siebel, Baan, J.D.Edwards, Oracle.
http://www.mmrc.com/

Print Jobs

Presented by Newhouse Associates, Print Jobs is a recruiter for printing and graphic arts industries. Their clients are Fortune 500 companies as well as some of the best small printing and graphic arts organizations in the USA. Print Jobs has been in business since 1985.
http://www.printjobs.com/

PrintLink

PrintLink is a Graphic Arts Professional Staffing Service for senior/middle print management and all digital prepress positions. With offices in the US and Canada, PrintLink serves a regional, national, and international market. PrintLink provides permanent placement opportunities for senior/middle print management, digital prepress, IT, and other key positions in the US and Canada.
http://printlink.com/

TempArt

TempArt is a Temporary Employment Agency for Ad Agencies, Graphic Design Firms, and Corporate Art Departments. TempArt Staffing has been a source for staffing professional creative talent for over 17 years. Ad Agencies, Design Firms, Corporate Marketing, and Web Departments place positions with them.
http://www.tempart.com/

Art Links Staffing

Art Links Staffing provides recruiting and temporary assistance for advertising, graphics, multimedia, and publishing. Their clients are businesses from Los Angeles to Vancouver, with primary concentration in the San Francisco Bay Area, where their home office is located. Marti Stites, a Certified Personnel Consultant, began ArtLinks in 1994 and continues as its working owner. She contributes 15 years of experience from Walnut Creek's Visual Arts Exhibition Program combined with prior work in human resources. http://www.artlinks-staffing.com/

AC Lion

Founded in 1996, AC Lion is an executive search firm for sales and technology for NY, Boston, LA, and San Francisco. AC Lion has done placements with over 150 different technology leaders, including some of the leading enterprise software development companies, infrastructure, data storage, network security, financial services, consulting services, and wireless companies. http://www.aclion.com

Digital People

Digital People, an advertising and marketing staffing company offering creative talent, media, and account service professionals, editors, illustrators, managers and talent in more than 22 other disciplines. The work they do includes contract; contract-to-hire; direct hire; long and short-term project; and illness and vacation coverage. The following represent the areas of employment they fill most frequently: Account Services, Art Director, Copywriter, Creative Director, Desktop Publisher, Graphic Designer, Media Planner/Buyer, Print Production, Project Manager, Web Content/Design, and

Web Production.
http://www.digipeople.com

PeopleWare

PeopleWare Technical Resources, Inc. is an agency specializing in the recruitment and placement of individuals in areas of the Internet, client/server and microsystem application development and support. PeopleWare® offers both contract and full-time employment opportunities. The staff has placed over 3,000 individuals and has done so without client advertising campaigns with the majority of their clients being software and hardware vendors developing products for the Internet, Windows, WIN95, NT, UNIX, Macintosh, and LAN environments.
http://www.peoplewareinc.com/

Planet Recruit

PlanetRecruit was formed in 1999 to help candidates in their search for a new career. The service is entirely free for job seekers—candidates can search for jobs, upload their resume—making it available to hundreds of recruitment agencies across the world—and register for job alerts which will email the candidate with any new jobs that match their requirements.
http://www.planetrecruit.com

Portfolios.com

Portfolios.com is a member of the BrandEra family of sites. This company is an online creative service that serves the needs of professionals in the marketing communications

industry. The company has been in business since 1995. They have many positions to offer in the arts.
http://www.portfolio.com/

Eagle Tech

EagleTech Consulting is a team of technical recruiters that conducts all of their business remotely or "virtually." They have developed an online, real-time database that allows all of their consultants to enter and share an unlimited number of job orders with each other. EagleTech Consulting was founded and is run by President and CEO, Ralph Toole.
http://www.eagletech.net

Brilliant People

Established in 1965, Management Recruiters International, Inc. (MRI) is a large executive search and recruitment organization, with more than 1,000 offices and 5,000 search professionals in North America, Europe and Asia. MRI provides a full range of employment services, from single searches for a key manager to major projects involving hundreds of assignments for a single-source client. In 2000, nearly 100,000 people worked on company assignments, including specialists in information technology, engineering and telecommunications, and in legal, administrative and office support. MRI placed another 45,000 people in a wide range of careers.
http://www.brilliantpeople.com

eXpertalent

eXpertalent is a WBENC and HUB certified woman-owned human capital management and consulting firm specialized in utilizing traditional recruiting methods as well as state-of-the-art, Internet based systems. The company provides employment to technical professionals as full-time employees—on a contingent fee basis—or as consultants. They provide their consultants with employment benefits including instant 401K participation, quality medical coverage, direct deposit, weekly payroll, and professional administrative support.
http://eXperTalent.com/

Big Fish

Big Fish provides staffing and consulting services for the creative, marketing, and digital media industries. If you are seeking a long-term advisor throughout your career, they have the resources to match your skills with some of the most exciting opportunities in the industry.
http://www.bigfishpromo.com

Creative Pro

If you color-correct images, run a printing press, or program a Web site, you are a creative professional. If you work in an ad agency, a service bureau, or (ahem) a vertical portal, you're a creative professional. Creative Pro research and placement coordinators contact top film, banking, advertising, Internet, sport, and PR companies on a daily basis, tracking down many hard-to-find positions.
http://www.creativepro.com/front/home

Creative Focus

Creative Focus, Inc. represents creative, advertising, and marketing professionals in Southern California. This firm represents graphic designers, creative/art directors, digital artists, production and traffic managers, etc. Their candidates are highly talented, some are award winning in their respective fields and above all have the experience and hands-on skillset that employers have come to expect.
http://www.focusstaff.com/index.html

Career Strategists

Career Strategists is owned and managed by Renee Peterson Trudeau. This company places individuals in positions throughout the country. An active leader in the Austin business community since 1990, Renee Peterson Trudeau has more than 14 years experience in career planning, marketing, and management. The passion for helping others realize their career dreams has been a driving force in her life and with the company.
http://www.careerstrategists.net/

Wet Feet

WetFeet, Inc. is a recruitment provider that helps companies attract, hire, and retain the right people. Corporate clients range from emerging high-growth companies to Fortune 1000 companies, including Merrill Lynch, KPMG Consulting, Federated Department Stores, The U.S. Navy, PricewaterhouseCoopers, Xerox, and Proctor & Gamble. Candidates rely on WetFeet's consumer Web sites for career-

related information.
http://www.wetfeet.com/asp/home.asp

CareerTrust

CareerTrust provides direct hire, full-time jobs in many
professional job categories including computer graphics and
animation. Clients include Fortune 500 and 1000 companies
who employ quality talent across the country. SearchLines is
utilized exclusively by CareerTrust's employment
professionals to show direct hire job opportunities.
http://www.careertrust.com/

CCI Network

Whatever your occupation, employed or unemployed, level
of education, industry experience, gender, race, religion,
national origin, family background, physical abilities, past
successes or failures, iThrive has something to add to the job
search. Referrals will come from your personal
relationships—friends, family and neighbors; people you
have worked with in the past; and the people you do business
with everyday. They have many opportunities for just about
anyone.
http://www.ccinetwork.com

Futurestep

Futurestep members, whose career profiles are instantly
available to global consultants, can apply for opportunities
and access valuable assessments to help manage their
careers. Futurestep is based in Los Angeles, California, and
has offices in more than 20 countries worldwide. This

company has been in business since 1998.
http://www.futurestep.com

Recruiter Connection

An eProfile contains your resume, cover-letter, and answers to commonly asked questions. Unlike an awkward phone call, your eProfile speaks for you, providing recruiters with the most relevant information in the shortest amount of time. RecruiterConnection provides exposure to recruiters, worldwide. Access over 3 million employment opportunities from over 310 top job sites, on one easy search page. With Apply Anywhere, it is easy to submit your eProfile to virtually any position you find.
http://www.RecruiterConnection.com

General Employment

General Employment has been in the business of finding career opportunities for people and people for career opportunities for over 100 years. The Company provides direct hire, contract, and contract-to-hire services through its network of offices in major metropolitan areas across the United States. They specialize in technology-related positions.
http://www.genp.com/

Headhunters.com

In 1988, Berkana International, Inc. was established to do high-tech recruiting for clients in France, Great Britain, and the United States. In 1995, having grown considerably by demonstrating respect for both candidate and client, Berkana launched an experiment: Headhunters.com. On this Web site there were listed executive openings in software companies as well as an impressive list of clients. With no subscriptions, registration forms, or passwords standing between job seekers and job posts Headhunters.com has the best service model for the long-term future. Find many job opportunities here.

http://www.headhunters.com

RitaSue Siegel Resources

A design executive search consulting firm where positions are listed for the entire country and abroad. The most important job they do is to help client companies find the best designers, design managers, and creative directors for their businesses. Client companies include: Apple Computer, Wolff Olins, Polaroid, Alta Vista, LVMH, Fitch, Nike, Philips Design (US, Europe, Asia,) Nokia, Nissan (Tokyo, US,) Rockwellgroup, Sony Interactive, Herbst Lazar Bell, Ford, Interbrand (US, Asia,) Emilio Ambasz, marchFIRST, Motorola, Landor, BBG/M, Lante, Mattel, KI, Renault, Barnes & Noble, Art Center College, Thomson Consumer Electronics, Group 4, Frassanito, IDI, Oh Boy!, Bergmeyer, Disney Interactive, Polo Ralph Lauren to name a few. Job postings are updated often.

http://www.ritasuesiegelresources.com/

Roz Goldfarb Associates

This is an agency that mostly deals with finding people for senior level jobs (design related); however, some starting/ production jobs are listed. Roz Goldfarb Associates

specializes in assisting creative businesses—in design, new media and advertising. RGA's clients include corporations, graphic design firms (including packaging, corporate identity firms, corporate literature, promotional design, annual reports), industrial design firms, advertising agencies, sales promotion and direct marketing agencies, marketing communications firms, publishing companies, media companies, retail and licensing firms, multimedia production and publishing companies, and online publications and services.
http://www.rga-joblink.com/docs/joblist.html

Susan Lee and Associates

Susan Lee is the founder and president of this recruiting firm. Prior to incorporating the business, she developed her network of contacts as a national sales executive for a printing equipment dealer. In addition, she has experience as the owner of a small publishing business. "Those years as a publishing business owner have been a valuable resource to me in evaluating the needs of my clients," Susan says. "I share their perspective; I know what's needed to manage the capital, financial, marketing, and employment requirements of a printing business."
http://www.susanlee.com/

Wert & Company

An international recruitment firm specializing in executive searches within the creative community. Wert & Company represents candidates in the following areas: Architecture, Interiors and Environments Brand Strategy Broadcast, Film and Video Business, Anthropology and Research, Corporate and Brand Identity, Editorial and Copywriting, Exhibit and Retail Store Design, Graphic Design, Industrial Design and Product Development, Information Architecture, Interaction Design, Interactive Media Marketing, and Creative Services Motion Graphics.

http://www.wertco.com/

Do-It-Yourself Outplacement

On this site, job seekers can post their resume where thousands of employers search. Employers can post job listings in the nation's largest online labor exchange, create customized job orders, and search resumes automatically to find the right people fast. Guided by the vision of America's Labor Market Information System, the U.S. Department of Labor (USDOL) has developed America's Career Kit in partnership with the states and private sector organizations. This powerful suite of Web-based tools includes AJB, America's Career InfoNet (ACINet) and America's Service Locator (ASL).

http://www.occ.com/occ/DoItYourself.html

Millennium Recruiters

Millennium Recruiters service a large list of established companies throughout California and across the country. They specialize in the pre-IPO, "Dot Com," recently IPO (issued within the last 12 months), and emerging "Cutting edge" companies. Visit their employment opportunities to see what is available.

http://www.millenniumrecruiters.com

High Tech Connect

HighTech Connect (HTC) specializes in placing marketing communications and public relations consultants for projects and interim staff assignments. With a network of more than 1200 experts, HighTech Connect provides client companies with targeted expertise in the areas of arts and communications. Subscribe to their mailing list and keep up-to-date on all the latest news and developments at HTC. http://www.htconnect.com

Testimonial

"It's great to know that HighTech Connect is there as extended staff when it's needed. HighTech's large database of highly-qualified consultants makes finding a match for an often very specialized need a quick and painless process."
        —Senior Manager of Worldwide Product Education, Sun Microsystems.

iJive.com

JobStar Canada Inc. is a privately owned Canadian Corporation with its head office in Calgary, Alberta, Canada. Their goal is to provide a place where job seekers, employers, and recruiters can easily connect. This company provides a career site that is easily navigable and user-friendly, uncluttered by a lot of flash or advertising. Since their launch in August of 1999 they have grown to be one of the most popular and most-visited career sites in Canada, boasting over 210,000 unique visitors to the site per month. http://www.ijive.com

General Job Sites

Dice.com

Job search Web site for computer professionals. Dice Inc. is an online provider of online recruiting services for technology professionals. Dice Inc. serves technology professionals and the companies that depend on them with services in recruiting and career development through dice.com and their job board. Dice won the first-ever WEDDLE's User's Choice Awards for Best Specialty Job Board for Recruiters and Best Specialty Job Board for Job Seekers.
http://www.dice.com/

Telecommunications Job Search

Search thousands of telecommunications jobs and post your resume. There are always media and art-related jobs on this site. Search by graphic design, by TV, or by film, and find listings that can't be found anywhere else. Currently contracted by over 500 leading telecommunications companies, TelecomCareers.Net is a complete online employment center.
http://www.telecomcareers.net/

Brain Hunter

On Brain Hunter job seekers will find thousands of jobs that are often not advertised elsewhere. There is never any charge

to job seekers, as all of the services are always free. Brain Hunter offers lots of services beyond the job board that will help with your job search.
http://www.Brainhunter.com/

Career Path

The Career Path site has employment listings from newspapers across the country. Over one hundred thousand jobs can be searched from all forms of employment including graphics and new media. Founded in 1995 under the name of NetStart Inc., the company developed careerbuilder.com and TeamBuilder software in 1996 and then developed TeamBuilder Online in 1997, the first browser-based recruiting application to accelerate the hiring process. In 1998, NetStart,Inc. was renamed CareerBuilder, Inc., and launched with 16 media and interactive partners.
http://www.careerpath.com/

NationJob Network

A general job search site and service. P.J. Scout can help job seekers search for a job right now—and keep up-to-date on any new jobs that match specific qualifications and interests by automatically e-mailing them on an ongoing basis. Enter your e-mail address so P.J. can send you new listings, free. You can still use the service, even without registering.
http://www.nationjob.com/

American Jobs

American Jobs lets candidates search jobs and post resumes for free. Additionally, they have thousands of human resource

Representatives and Recruiters signed up to search resumes, so post your resume before you leave the site. AmericanJobs.com is recognized by Fortune Magazine, CareerXroads, Weddles, and The Recruiters Bible as one of the most cost effective employment sites on the net to post jobs and search resumes. There are over 350,000 resumes online.
http://www.americanjobs.com/

America's Job Bank

Job seekers can post their resume where thousands of employers search every day, search for job openings automatically, and find a job fast. Employers can post job listings in the nation's largest online labor exchange, create customized job orders, and search resumes automatically to find the right people fast. Guided by the vision of America's Labor Market Information System, the U.S. Department of Labor (USDOL) has developed America's Career Kit in partnership with the states and private sector organizations. Find lots of government jobs here.
http://www.ajb.dni.us/

CareerResources.Net

The Career Resource Homepage has become a big resource for finding employment on the Web. It has been widely quoted in various articles, including the Wall Street and Financial World. It has also been reviewed in various online resources such as Magellian-Mckinley's Internet Directory, iGuide Net Review, Internet Business 500 by Ventana Communications Group, and New Rider's Official World

Wide Web Yellow Pages. Find lots of low-key jobs here with smaller businesses and corporations.
http://www.careerresource.net/

HotJobs

HotJobs.com, a subsidiary of Yahoo!, is a recruiting solutions and software company. The company's flagship job site, HotJobs.com was voted the "Best General Purpose Job Board for Job Seekers" in a survey of job seekers conducted by WEDDLE's. The company recently ranked #14 in Bloomberg Personal Finance Magazine's coveted "Tech 100" list. Find many art and media-related jobs on this site as well as many other "hot" resources.
http://www.hotjobs.com

Monster.com

A general job posting site with additional information about resumes and job searching. Be sure to look at their thought provoking commercial "The Road Not Taken." Enter your desired job information and search the huge Monster database. Use your Monster resume to quickly apply online. Learn more about these exclusive job search and career management tools that power you ahead of your competition.
http://www.monster.com

NationJob

A closely-held private company based in Des Moines, Iowa, NationJob owns and operates NationJob Network. This network of Internet sites and services is consistently ranked

among the top employment sites on the Web. NationJob's value-added services include a network of Specialty Sites promoting jobs in specific employment categories including computer graphics and animation.
http://www.nationjob.com/

Guru

Guru combines a mixture of science, technology, and human interaction to deliver employment opportunities for those artists seeking contract employment. Candidates in the Guru process undergo skill and cultural assessments. They provide you with contract and permanent job opportunities, career guidance, and support services. Plus, the talent agents and online tools enable you to find your ideal position based on your expertise and work-style preferences.
http://www.guru.com

Career Builder

Career Builder offers the a recruitment resource through more than 130 local newspapers, reaching a combined Sunday print circulation of more than 15 million readers and more than 26 million unique visitors to its newspaper Web sites online each month. In November, 2001, Career Builder acquired Headhunter.net which bolstered its strength online, extended its market reach and enhanced its overall technical capabilities. Find lots of opportunities on this all-purpose job board.
http://www.careerbuilder.com

Computer Jobs

Founded in 1995, the company provides its visitors with computer-related job opportunities and career-related content organized into 18 vertical skill sets and 19+ major metropolitan markets. More than 4,000 companies post jobs to ComputerJobs.com including IBM, Microsoft, UPS, The Home Depot, Georgia-Pacific, Coca-Cola Corporation, BellSouth Corporation, Chick-fil-A, E&Y, Deloitte and Touche, Southern Company, Hall Kinion, Comsys, Matrix, Spherion, and Ciber.
http://www.computerjobs.com/

Flip Dog

FlipDog.com delivers the Internet's largest job collection—all direct from the source—employer Web sites. This company gets jobs from five times more employers each week than other job sources do in a year because of the research they do. There are jobs from big and small companies, public and private organizations, or anywhere at all. FlipDog.com presents a comprehensive directory of jobs found on the Web.
http://www.flipdog.com

Job Circle

JobCircle is an online recruitment tool that provides careers, content, and community to technology, telecomm, and engineering professionals. JobCircle.com currently operates in CT, DC, DE, OH, MD, NY, NJ, PA, VA, and WV, and provides a totally regional job search experience using their Latitude/Longitude functionality. They provide a plethora of features that make it easy for an employer to post classified ads, and by creating a simple resume submission process. http://www.jobcircle.com

National Search

With 10,000-12,000 help-wanted display ads from the newspapers of 60 large metropolitan areas from across the U.S. that are updated weekly, job seekers are bound to find something here. This search company is geared toward the Managerial Professional Executive and Technical segment of the workforce. Searchable by discipline-locationdate. Since 1970, the newspaper version of the National Ad Search has provided coverage of job opportunities in the nation. http://www.nationaladsearch.com

Brassring

Brassring provides jobs, advice, articles, and many other career resources. As a first-time user, just follow a few simple steps and you will quickly be on your way to a job search and tech knowledge. They will e-mail jobs that match your qualifications directly to your e-mail account on a daily, weekly, or monthly basis and post and store up to 5 different resumes and cover letters. http://www.1-Jobs.com/recruiters/job-search-agent.htm

Testimonials

"Of all the job Web sites I was on, BrassRing was the most effective for me. I was able to land more interviews off of my BrassRing resume than any other."

—Job Seeker.

"This site is a great addition to the many other beneficial sites for job seeking and recruiters. I appreciate the work put into this one. It was

very straightforward and to the point. Again, thanks for a site that is committed to reaching those of us who need to stay in contact with the technology of the town and even the world."

—Job Seeker.

4Work

4Work offers search tools for job seekers and tools that help you pinpoint exactly what you are looking for. Plus, 4Work sponsors http://www.4LaborsofLove.org, The Internet Volunteer Initiative, dedicated to making the world a better place by helping volunteers and non-profit organizations find each other.
http://www.4work.com/

Brain Buzz

BrainBuzz.com offers IT jobs, skills training, professional certification, career enhancement, and peer tech support. They are one of the top five career information Web sites on the Internet as rated by Top9.com, plus they are 100% dedicated to serving the IT professional. BrainBuzz.com was designed by IT professionals, for IT professionals—and they are "The IT Career Network." Post your resume on the BrainBuzz.com Job Seekers community, where employers can browse them.
http://www.Brainbuzz.com

Career.com

Launched in 1993, Career.com is the first "Dot Com" recruitment advertising service. Career.com has a history of online HR support innovations such as: Interactive recruiting, Hot Jobs a special feature to showcase critical jobs,

Job Hosting, CyberFair, Virtual Job Fair & JobDigger. Career.com also known in the industry, as HEART Advertising is a privately held woman owned business incorporated in the state of California.
http://www.career.com/

True Careers

TrueCareers serves large Fortune 1000 businesses and over one million candidates nationwide. As an industry expert in employment issues, TrueCareers has been quoted often by leading news sources such as USA Today, CNN and BusinessWeek. Nearly 90% of TrueCareers users have a college degree, and average 6 years of experience. TrueCareers recruits candidates with the help of Sallie Mae, its parent company and the nation's leader in student loan financing. TrueCareers taps Sallie Mae's 7 million plus borrowers to fill its candidate pool.
http://www.careercity.com/

WorkTree

WorkTree is a large job search portal. They provide job seekers with links to the thousands of job sites & resources on the Internet. Thousands of job sites and career resources have been pre-researched and indexed by them. Their goal is to provide the online job seeker with the access and knowledge needed to get a more complete picture of the huge hidden job market on the Web. No one job site can claim to have all the jobs on the Web. But Worktree.com claims to have nearly all the job sites/resources that have nearly all the jobs on the Web.
http://www.worktree.com/

Career Matrix

CareerMatrix.com is not an employment agency. CareerMatrix.com is a free resource for job seekers. Post a resume or search for a new job from a large selection of direct hire positions from leading Midwest companies. When you have found an opportunity, send your resume, directly to the human resource representative. Simply click the "Send My Resume" button at the bottom of every job posting. Sign up for Job Alert, it's free. Anytime a company posts a new job, receive e-mail notification so you can quickly respond to an employers needs.

http://www.careermatrix.com

Career Span

Search the database of thousands of current employer and recruiter posted openings by keyword, location, education required, and more. You can post your resume and apply for jobs with the click of a button. Resumes may be posted as public (employer searchable), confidential (employer searchable, identity concealed with blind email contact) or private (not employer searchable-used only by you to apply for jobs). If you'd like more exposure, you can spotlight your resume with additional features where your resume is displayed to employers when searching before basic resumes. Premium resumes may be posted as public (employer searchable) or confidential.

http://www.careerspan.com

Employment Spot

This free resource center offers a high-utility collection of top employment-related sites. From EmploymentSpot.com, quickly and easily find job-seeking sites, salary and benefits information, resume- and job-posting opportunities, company profiles, internships, career glossaries, job banks, interviewing tips, and much more.

http://www.employmentspot.com/

Testimonial

"Time for a career change? Employment Spot helps you find the nation's fastest growing occupations, then leads you to online resources to track them down."

—USA Today.

Free Agent

Millions of men and women are choosing to become consultants, freelancers, independent contractors— professional free agents. As a free agent, you decide how to blend work and life. At Freeagent.com, job seekers will find plenty of work in the computer graphics and animation industries.

http://www.FreeAgent.com

Freelance.com

Following a start in the Information Technology business, Freelance.com is now expanding its activities into advertising and consulting. Freelance.com management team is led by Eric Delannoy. Eric is based in Paris, France. Freelance.com offers many opportunities for the professional who is looking

to work freelance.
http://www.freelance.com

Helpwanted.com

Here, the profile information job seekers enter in you account is matched with all new employer job postings. Job postings that match your profile are automatically placed in the "New Job Postings" section of "My Job Manager." The "My Job Manager" module lets job seekers view jobs saved during a prior job search session, view job postings applied for, and view all new job postings that meet the criteria selected in the profile.
http://www.helpwanted.com

Jobs.net

Candidates from all corners of the planet can search for jobs locally or internationally. The search engine at Jobs.net can pinpoint the jobs that suit you based on keywords, skills, location, experience, educational background, schedule, salary, benefits, etc. Jobs.NET provides tips, advice, and techniques in helping candidates find satisfying employment.
http://www.jobs.net/

Job Bank USA

Since 1995 JobBankUSA.com has provided services to over 5 million job seekers, hiring managers, recruiters, and human resource professionals. Candidates have the ability to identify and apply for positions. All candidates are given access to tools designed to help put together an effective resume and to

mount an efficient search for a desired position.
http://www.jobbankusa.com/

Jobfind.com

Locate a job by searching through job postings of employers. Use a simple criteria builder to create searches. Quickly find jobs that meet your exact specifications. Apply immediately to any job postings that interest you or save your search criteria for later use. Post an attractive easy-to-design Web (HTML) resume with graphics and hyperlinks using these features or use the jobfind Resume Builder to create your resume or just cut and paste your existing resume for quick and simple entry. You will receive immediate, automatic email notification when an employer requests an interview. Jobfind.com notifies you when a job meets your specifications. http://www.jobfind.com

Job Link, USA, Inc.

Job Link USA, Inc. works to help college grads find employment. Job Link USA, Inc. is currently located in the Northwest Region of Chicago, IL, but offers employment nationwide. Send your resume in today and start receiving employment opportunities tomorrow.
http://www.joblink-usa.com

Testimonials

"Who would have ever thought that I would land a career within my major two months prior to graduating from college. I received over twenty responses within just one week after putting my resume

---

online. Keep up the good work Job Link USA."

—Job Seeker.

"After trying Job Link USA for a month, I must say that I was impressed with the number of responses I received from companies not only in my city, but all around the USA in a short period of time. I now work for one of the leading Stock Brokers in the Country. Thanks, Job Link USA."

—Job Seeker.

JobsOnline

JobsOnline provides job seekers with extensive job listings and useful career resources to begin a successful job search. Thousands of jobs, resume and cover letter samples, expert career advice, and a handy salary calculator are available to job seekers. Let their career expert give you advice on all sorts of employment related issues. Figure out what you are worth and then negotiate your new salary by using their handy salary calculator.
http://www.jobsonline.com

Job-Search-Engine

Job-Search-Engine.com has launched new services for job seekers and recruiters. My.Job-Search-Engine.com provides a resume posting service, job search agents, and a job leads tool. Ten new job sites, including FlipDog.com and Hotjobs.com, are also available for meta-searching. Users can also search 110 English and French Canadian job boards simultaneously. European users now have a job search engine that searches the top 60 job boards from the United Kingdom.
http://www.job-search-engine.com/

Job Search Link

Job Search Link has divided their site into logical sections to help make the job search less time-consuming. For instance, instead of having to navigate from site to site to look up sample interview questions, you can simply click "Interviewing" to find links that take you directly to interview questions. As you browse through this site, you will find that every section has links to samples and tips. Also find many job postings here.
http://www.jobsearchlink.com/

Jobwarehouse

All services for Job Seekers are always 100% free. Advertise your resume, search thousands of high quality jobs, visit specific hiring companies, and let them help you in making your career search a great success.
http://www.jobwarehouse.com/

JobWeb

To research employers, most college students use a combination of print and electronic resources. The numbers confirm it: In a recent online survey by the National Association of Colleges and Employers (NACE), 78 percent of responding students said they gather employer information from both print publications and Web sites. NACE offers access to graduating college students through its Job Choices publications and its JobWeb site.
http://www.jobWeb.com

Megajob site

WorkLife designs, develops, installs, hosts, and manages career management sites for its customers. In 1995, WorkLife created one of the first online career centers for Microsoft's MSN, aggregating more than 50 leading career, human resources and entrepreneur brands all under one unified site. In 1998 WorkLife launched AltaVista's first Career Channel and now WorkLife is powering over 175 different career and employer channels. WorkLife has brought together more than 30 of the Web's leading employment industry brands including most major job boards to offer the first unified search for job seekers, employers, and the self-employed for fresh content, jobs, and resumes.
http://www.megajob site.com/

Net-Temps

Net-Temps is consistently ranked in the top 10 job posting Web sites based on traffic by Media Metrix and Nielsen// Net Ratings. Net-Temps' service provides a means for staffing agencies to take advantage of electronic recruiting. For Job Seekers, Net-Temps provides a convenient and free method to post resumes, inquire about available positions and apply for jobs online. Media Metrix, Fortune Magazine, 100hot.com, PC World and PC Week all rank Net-Temps in the top ten on the basis of traffic out of an estimated 25,000 Web sites with job postings.
http://www.net-temps.com/

Professional Jobs

Fill in the career profile to have your credentials considered for top-level openings with the nation's leading employers and recruiters, including the highest-level income positions in all fields and industries nationwide. If confidentiality is crucial, you can specify at the end of the form that your name and e-mail address be blocked. Your membership will also give you instant free access to openings along with job seeking counsel.
http://www.professionaljobs.com

Thingamajob

Thingamajob is an employment resource with many job postings. It is a free online employment tool with many resources that extend beyond the job board. They offer a wide spectrum of job opportunities and employment that include TEKsystems, Mentor 4, and Onsite Companies, Inc.
http://www.thingamajob.com

Job Next

JobNext is the only Internet site that offers its career match services for free to both job seekers and employers. Launched in November 2000, with a staff of four, Alabama based JobNext has grown to include 16 people with offices in US and correspondence in Canada, UK, France, Japan, and Hong Kong. Find many job opportunities here.
http://www.jobnext.com

JOB.com

Job.com recently announced that USJobBoard.com surpassed the one million unique visitor mark for the first time recently. Founded in 2001, Job.com, Inc. owns and operates one of the fastest growing career sites. They offer unlimited resume searching, and unlimited Job Ad Posting, on a monthly subscription basis. They offer candidates a wide selection to choose from.
http://www.job.com

Employment 911

Established in 1997, Employment911.com is a resource for job seekers, recruiters, and employers. Employment911.com was launched with the idea to provide an "all in one" solution for job seekers recruiters and employers. Not only Employment911's job postings are searched but also currently over 3,000,000 jobs in over 300 major career sites are also simultaneously searched. Job seekers even have an option of retrieving their email over the phone.
http://www.employment911.com

Vault

Fortune recently called Vault, "the best place on the Web to prepare for a job search." Vault offers insider company information, advice, and career management services. Vault's career content includes information on over 3,000 companies and 70 industries. Vault's Electronic WaterCooler is the Internet's first collection of company-specific message boards for employees. Every day, tens of thousands of people visit Vault's expert-moderated message boards to share the latest corporate and career news, network with each other, ask for job advice and learn about trends shaping the workforce. Vault.com's free resume service allows users to post their resumes and be contacted by potential employers. And the job board contains hundreds of postings for creative job seekers.

http://www.vault.com/

Media Bistro

Mediabistro.com is a job site for anyone that works to create content in a creative way. That includes editors, writers, television producers, graphic designers, book publishers, people in production, and circulation departments—in industries including magazines, television, radio, newspapers, book publishing, online media, advertising, PR, and graphic design. They provide both on and offline employment opportunities.

http://www.mediabistro.com/

Job Pilot

The company launched its jobpilot Internet site in October 1995. Sites are now online in 15 European countries, as well as sites in Asia, Australia and the USA. Jobpilot is an e-recruitment provider. Jobpilot is based in Bad Homburg, Germany, which is near Frankfurt. European subsidiaries are located in Austria, Belgium, the Czech Republic, Denmark, France, Hungary, Italy, the Netherlands, Norway, Poland, Spain, Sweden, Switzerland, and the United Kingdom.

http://www.jobpilot.com

Job Circle

JobCircle.com has been voted as one o the "TOP 50" career sites in the 2002 edition of CareerXRoads and they just got voted one of the TOP 100 fastest growing privately held companies in Philadelphia by the Wharton School of Business and the Philadelphia Business Journal. JobCircle.com provides regional employment opportunities, resume submission, career development, monthly columns, discussion databases, tech news, regional career events to creative and technology individuals seeking employment.
http://www.jobcircle.com

Quintessential Careers

Quintessential Careers is a career, job, and college site, offering free expert career and job-seeking advice (through articles, tools, tips, and tutorials), as well as links to all the best job sites. Special sections for teens, college students, and all other job seekers (by industry, geography, and job-seeker type) are also available.
http://www.quintcareers.com/US_job_resources.html

US Careers

US Careers Resource Center is a full line employment and resource center specializing in the Engineering, Computer and Business industries. At US Careers, the services are paid for by advertisers and client companies. They house hundreds of positions in their search engine and they also provide the option of posting your resume—for free—to the large and small corporations in the United States.
http://www.uscareers.com/

A2Zmoonlighter.com

Since 2000, this company has helped art professionals find work with some of the largest companies around. Corporations like Fujitsu, Siemens, and McGraw Hill. Basic Membership is free for professionals; however, they offer Choice subscription memberships to serious and quality professionals to set themselves apart and get tangible benefits such as guaranteed project leads, and more.
http://www.A2Zmoonlighter.com/

BrainBid

BrainBid is for those job seekers that want contract employment. BrainBid matches employers having project work with free agents. BrainBid members enjoy an online sealed bid process. This Web system also includes the Internet's first online status tracking engine for employers and free agents. If you are looking for contract work, BrainBid has plenty of it.
http://www.brainbid.com

eWork

eWork is located is headquartered in San Francisco with additional offices throughout the United States and in Europe. While most of their listings are freelance or contract, there are some listings for full-time employment with a lot creative listings.
http://www.ework.com

Freelancers.com

The classified ads /help wanted section presents ads posted by them, but also open to all employers for a nominal charge. Responses to paid ads are sent directly to the employer. Enter your background/resume information in new candidates. This is the database consulted when their company and others are looking for specific skills. If you wish, you can add a single image to your resume for $25. Lots of listings for creative work.

http://www.freelancers.com/

ComputerJobs.com

The company provides its visitors with computer-related job opportunities and career-related content organized into 18 vertical skill sets and 19+ major metropolitan markets. More than 4,000 companies post jobs to ComputerJobs.com including IBM, Microsoft, UPS, The Home Depot, Georgia-Pacific, Coca-Cola Corporation, BellSouth Corporation, Chick-fil-A, E&Y, Deloitte and Touche, Southern Company, Hall Kinion, Comsys, Matrix, Spherion, and Ciber. ComputerJobs.com is a privately held Atlanta-based corporation with investments from Internet Capital Group (NASDAQ: ICGE) and Mellon Ventures.

http://www.carolina.computerjobs.com/

Developers.net

Developers.net, a service of Tapestry.Net, is completely confidential and free for job seekers. Developers.net members receive jobs by email matching their personal expertise and desired job location and notifies applicants by email when hiring companies review their resumes. Developers.net features U.S.-based Information Technology jobs from companies including Microsoft, Cabletron/ Enterasys, Southwest Airlines, and many others. http://www.developers.net

Computerwork.com

"High Tech Jobs for High Tech Professionals," a job search Web site for computer professionals. Owned by Internet Association Group, Inc. in Jacksonville, Florida, Computerwork.com was established in 1995 to serve the needs of both computer professionals seeking employment and staffing firms and corporations seeking IT candidates. The tools for job seekers such as Job Tracker, Resume Tracker, and Saved Searches compare favorably with the tools offered by much larger, less focused job boards. http://www.computerwork.com/

FindCreative.com

FindCreative.com is a job search and job posting Web site designed for the creative community. Additional information and forum relating to the creative job search is available. Because their marketing campaign is strictly targeted to the creative community, Findcreative.com offers lots of listing in the arts. Find full-time employment as well as contract work. http://www.findcreative.com/

International Job Sites

Agency Central UK

Spanning over 40 industries, Agency Central allows job seekers to find many opportunities in the UK. Additional features include a Secure CV Database, Industry Bodies, Media Sources, and Career Advice.
http://www.agencycentral.co.uk/

Asia Net

Established in 1997, Asia-Net has been serving Asia/Pacific-Rim business communities by helping professionals locate job opportunities. The Asia-Net community comprises over 140,000 professionals with professional interests in Asia/Pacific-Rim. Find lots of opportunities in Asia.
http://www.asia-net.com/

Asian Career Web

Asian Career Web is the U.S. subsidiary of Recruit Co., Ltd., one of the largest publishers in Japan and a leader in the employment information industry. This company specializes in assisting multinational corporations to recruit Japanese-English bilingual employees to staff their global operations. Asian Career Web provides lots of listings for overseas employment.
http://www.rici.com/acw/ Recruit I.C.I.

Hong Kong Jobs

Since June 1996, HKJobs.com has been providing job opportunities in the Hong Kong region. HKJobs.com provides tools that help both employers and job seekers. Special features include: Job Search by various criteria, Quick Application, Job Alert, Online Resume Posting, MyHKJobs, My Job Board, and Career Resources.
http://www.hkjobs.com/

JobServe

JobServe allows users to search for jobs in the UK. Type in a keyword such as "graphics" or "photoshop" for the job search. The Jobserve search builder has been designed to make sure you can find the jobs you are interested in quickly and easily. It enables you to build up your search using the suggested keywords or by entering your own, therefore indicating exactly what you want and what you don't want.
http://www.jobserve.com/

Job site UK

GoJob site is the UK's leading Internet recruitment service. They set up in 1995 and were the UK's first multi-sector online recruitment site. They were awarded 'Best E-cruitment Service' by judges of the Professional Recruiter Awards for Excellence 2002, and in September 2001, GoJob site was voted the best UK multi-sector site in the National Online Recruitment Awards. They are also the only UK online recruiter to be awarded "EBrandLeader" status by the Superbrands Council. There are plenty of jobs on this site if

you live or are planning to live in the UK.
http://www.job site.co.uk/

MacWorld UK JobFinder

Select from three art/design job categories and what part of
the UK (or the entire country). All the jobs listed here can be
searched and sorted using the search bar at the top of the
screen. You may search by: Selecting the category of positions
your search falls in to. Selecting the geographical area that
you wish to search in. Typing a specific keyword for the jobs
you require. Then hit the "Search now" button. Using this
search tool will allow you to find the right job for you quickly
and easily.
http://www.macworld.co.uk/jobfinder/

MAYA International

Maya International is one of London's Internet and New
Media Recruitment consultancies. Their site offers Internet
and New Media jobs and has a database of key links for the
Internet and New Media professional. They offer three
service divisions: Permanent: catering for all permanent
Internet and New Media positions Freelance: placement of
contracting staff, on a short or long-term basis Consultant &
Executive: offering an executive search and selection service
and the placement of specialist consultants.
http://www.maya.co.uk/

Network Design

Network Design offers placement services for graphic design,
interior design, design management, architecture, and

product design positions. Located in London, most of the positions are in the United Kingdom. They offer many positions but specifically in the areas of Architecture and Interior Design, Graphic Design and Design Management, and the ever-emerging New Media sector.
http://www.networkdesign.cc/frameset.htm

RecruitMedia

RecruitMedia offers design, electronic imaging, and new media related jobs in the UK. Recruit Media was launched by Managing Director, Victoria Lubbock in 1989. A former journalist and editor, the idea behind the company was to build a talent base of editorial and design staff available for both short-term projects and permanent employment in the creative, media, and business information sectors.
http://www.recruitmedia.co.uk/

An Interview with Michael R. Mizen

President and Owner of Mizen & Associates, Inc—a

Technology Based Training and Interactive Presentations

Company

More companies are using decision support systems that administer questionnaires online or at a kiosk in the personnel office, combine the answers with a digital resume, and make a decision based on preset parameters. How do job applicants benefit from this system and how does an artist showcase samples of his/her creative portfolio in this environment?

Two different questions. Use the kiosk for hard skills assessment; artists cannot be judged in this environment. Chopin would likely get tossed in the kiosk but if you listened to his music you would have a different impression.

Networking is about establishing informal relationships with other people, people who can provide information that can help in the job search. How does one find out about these networking meetings and how can applicants use networking to find the right job without being too pushy?

Locally- newspapers/local newspapers. If there are specific interests then use the Internet for searching and hone the location to "multimedia in Chicago" and you will get the AMC, IEC, etc. Also register for the large job pools like monster.com, grassisgreener.com

What are the benefits/drawbacks to including temp work or an internships on your resume?

Benefits depend on where you are in your career. Just starting these help define your interests and the fact that you are building your skills. Later in career could indicate you are changing careers and are taking steps to prove this. But too much temp work might send a message about being a potential "problem hire;" why can't they get a straight job…"

How can a recruiter help applicants that have little or no job experience, and what should their first step be?

Have a plan and execute and be patient. "Internet Time" is not longer popular and probably was not ever real.

What are the advantages to searching for a job online? What are some of the drawbacks?

Selection, selection, selection. However it is the quality of the description. If there are so many positions what are the disadvantages?

Should an applicant follow up the resume with a 'did you get it' phone call or what should their next step be after sending their resume?

Basics 101-yes.

What are some of the things one should never say or do during a jobinterview?

Stress the positive; do not burn bridges, and remember that what you speak is like an e-mail; it may stick around and come back later.

Do job-seeking practices change for someone re-entering the job market?

Figure out why you left and how you are going to explain getting back in. It is a bigger question as you grow older and/or are moving into new careers (my present one is #4 and I expect at least 2 more if I can stay healthy).

What kinds of advantages do students finishing schools now have over those that entered the job market say ten years ago?

Newer skill sets in demand. I am not proficient in JAVA but new grads are going to be. Plus their ability to get information as a skill is better although I think my age/experience allows me better insight. This later aspect is probably challengeable as well.

Michael R. Mizen, Treasurer, AMC
Mizen & Associates, Inc.
River Forest, IL 60305 USA
Technology Based Training Interactive Presentations

Job Search Strategies

It takes strategy and good planning to be good at anything. And the job search process is certainly no different. Job seekers need to know what they want if they expect to get it. Below, find some strategies that will aid in the job search and help job seekers land the job that's right for them.

Identify Promising Organizations

According to a study by CareerXRoads, "most successful job-search contacts made online in 2001 happened directly at corporate Web sites, not through job boards." Why? It's simple. Organizations don't like to pay the advertising costs of most job boards. Instead, they'll post most of their jobs on their Web site and only pay to advertise their hard-to-fill jobs. The rest of their job openings may be posted to their Web site. Job seekers may think this is a simple concept and that's correct. But it's also the most overlooked strategy for landing a good job.

The first step should be to identify promising organizations that may be hiring. Do this by asking yourself a few simple questions. Am I looking for work in a particular industry? Do I want to work in a particular geographic area? Am I seeking employers offering a particular set of benefits or opportunities, such as good training or mentoring, opportunities for quick advancement, or perhaps a generous retirement plan?

A good way to identify promising organizations is to check out some of the Web sites listed in this book. For example, Vault.com, Wetfeet.com, and Employment911.com. All of these sites offer inside tips on companies and how employers are doing their hiring. Although there may not be job listings of interest on these employment sites, job seekers will find key contact info. Try to identify the manager for whom you would work and send a resume directly to that person, as well as to Human Resources. Go the extra mile in tracking down information about the company. And call the HR department to see about setting up informational interviews with current employees. Most often, your efforts will be rewarded and the company will be impressed by your initiative and interest by granting your request for an interview.

Job seekers should also be sure to read appropriate magazines and journals that will alert readers of key changes within the industry. These periodicals can give you the inside edge that you need to get in. Don't overlook any little piece of information. Every little bit helps when an edge is what you need.

Once a list of employers has been identified, visit their Web sites. There job seekers will find a much larger range of listings than on Monster.com or other employment sites. If there aren't any listings, email a resume anyway and ask about any possible openings.

Above all, be proactive. Don't wait for the job to fall into your lap, go and find it.

Use Networking Contacts

By far, contacts are the best way to land jobs. Some of the best jobs out there are never even advertised at all. Networking opens the door to a lot of job openings that would never come about otherwise. In addition, by networking job seekers can learn a lot about breaking into their chosen career field, identify top employers, and meet some great people in the process.

Networking is a large part of how the world works today. Networking with professionals in the arts can help job seekers in three ways. First off, contacts can offer insight that will help with the job search because they've been there. Secondly, since they work in the field, they may know about the "hidden job market" and could be your ticket in. And the networking process continues to help job seekers even after landing a job. Building relationships with mentors and professional associations will all help to achieve long-term career goals.

The Principles of Networking

Networking contacts are helpful for many reasons, but job seekers should establish these relationships for the right reasons. Ask for help, but don't ask them to help you find a job. There are several reasons for this. First, if your contact is not in a position to hire, or if they don't know of any appropriate job openings, that's usually the end of the discussion. You've asked for a job (or for job leads), they don't have any, they're busy, they need to get back to work. Not to mention the fact that you don't want to ask someone you barely know to go out on a limb for you. It's just not good business. You need to build a good foundation on which to grow. However, once you've established a relationship with your network contact, use the relationship to your advantage. Mention that you are job seeking, give them a copy of your resume, or ask for names of others in the industry. But by all means, job seekers should keep it casual and make sure to keep the contact. It should never be about using people or stepping on people, but about people helping each other. Offer to do something for your network contact in exchange for anything they can do for you. You are not trying to hide the fact that you are looking for a job so it is okay to ask, "What is the best way to apply for a position with this organization," or "What are good organizations to target for jobs in this field."

Be Persistent

Life is filled with challenges—constantly—and only those that are diligent in their pursuits will win. If you want to land the job of your dreams, you've got to push yourself beyond your comfort zone. If you aren't willing to put yourself out there to make the contacts, you can't expect to get anywhere fast. Expect challenges. Know that not all leads will actually lead you somewhere. Phone numbers change, corporations downsize, people move, there will be setbacks. But if you accept them as part of the process, it will be much easier to move on to the next step. And that's finding another way, another contact, another lead.

Some Ways to Network

Professional association meetings and conferences are a great way for job seekers to learn about trends, make new connections, and find out about job opportunities.

Professionally affiliated listservs and newsgroups, http://www.liszt.com/, can connect networks of professionals within a career field by computer. Listservs and newsgroups are used by professionals to gather information, share opinions, and even disseminate job listings. MentorNet.net, http://www.mentornet.net/, is another great place to make contacts in the field.

Be Organized in Your Job Search

While searching for employment, job seekers will be meeting lots of people, sending out tons of resumes, and corresponding with lots of employers. If you don't keep all this information organized, you're bound to get off track. At the end of this book, you'll find a great record-keeping system that will help you with this task.

Staying In Touch

Remember, networking is about establishing relationships with people long-term. Networking is also a mutual exchange—job seekers should also try to do something for the employer. Don't throw away a valuable connection by not staying in touch with the contact. Send a thank you note within a day or two of meeting with the contact. And keep your contacts informed of your progress. Network contacts will want to know how things are going. If somebody referred you to another contact who was particularly helpful, write to the original person and let them know.

Temp Jobs

Many people find excellent, full-time, long-term positions through their temp jobs. Temping allows job seekers to make a livable salary while they size up the company prior to making a commitment. Many temp agencies now specialize in particular career fields, and a new trend, "executive temping," has emerged in the last few years, allowing people with established career credentials to make a good income while filling temporary roles. While finding your niche in the arts, temping may be a viable solution. It gets your foot into the door and allows you to gain some excellent experience while finding long-term employment.

Career and Job Fairs

Career and job fairs offer the opportunity to meet many employers at one time. Before attending, be sure you know what employers will be there and what types of jobs they may be offering. Also, it is important to know if the employers will actually be conducting interviews onsite, or if this is simply an opportunity to speak with employers and exchange your resume for their business cards and literature. Below, find some great resources for finding career and job fairs.

CareerCity Online Job Fairs

Select a city, then review the local listings in the virtual employer booths. http://www.careercity.com/fair/

Career Conferences

Major career fairs for American and foreign-born students and alumni. http://www.careerconferences.com/

CareerFair.com

Online virtual career fair for college graduates. http://www.careerfair.com/

Career Fairs.com

High-tech, professional, sales, and college job fairs. http://www.careerfairs.com/careerfairs/default.htm

Career Mosaic Online Job Fairs

Virtual job fairs with specific employers. http://www.careermosaic.com/cm/cm35.html

CareerShop.com

Over 40 online job fairs organized by location, resume posting, and links to a library of employers. http://www.careershop.com/mainjfpg.asp

E*Fair.net

Online information technology job fairs. http://www.efair.net/index.cfm?veaction=jobseeker

Job Fairs

Nationwide job fairs sorted by type of position http://www.hrlive.com/local-bin/trajfc.cgi

JobsAmerica

Career fairs all over. Claims to be "the nation's leading producer of non-engineering job fairs." http://www.jobsamerica.com/

JobWeb

Provides an extensive database of college-oriented job fairs. http://www.jobWeb.org/search/cfairs

Premier Show Management

Job Fairs around the country. Job seekers who are in a different geographic area can also submit their resume. http://www.premiershow.com/fairs.htm

PSI Job Fairs

Technical, professional, and diversity Job Fairs at US locations. From Personnel Strategies, Inc. http://www.psijobfair.com/jobfairs.html.

Resume Databases

Resume databases can be a great way for job seekers to get their name out there, but it can be a time-consuming project and sometimes there's very little payoff. On the one hand, people in a wide variety of career fields attract good job leads this way. But on the other hand, the forms that a lot of employment sites are using can be tedious and lengthy. It's often a painful process to turn your resume into something their form will accept. The best sites let job seekers upload their resume as is, or cut and paste it into forms.

Most resume databases are free and the large commercial resume databases are easy to locate. But a lot of the time, the smaller art-specific Web sites are more effective to finding employment. In either case, job seekers need to be able to play the keyword game. If a resume does not contain at least some of the keywords that employers are using to search the database, then it will be skipped by the computer, even it contains all of the experience and skills required by the job. Later in this book, readers will learn more about keywords and how to use them to their advantage.

Some resume databases now offer you an "upgrade" for resumes, charging a fee so that a resume is in front of others who do not pay the fee. Don't pay for something you can get for free. Employment sites can't guarantee that a "paying" resume will be seen any time before one that is getting there for free.

Resume Resources

JobStar.org, Topics include "Descriptions of Major Resume Banks," "Should You or Shouldn't You? Evaluating Resume Banks," and "Let's Get Electronic: Why Employers Use Resume Banks." http://jobstar.org/Internet/res-main.htm.

How2FindaJob.com, Complete their resume form, and their software will take your information and post it field by field to the top 30 job boards. There is a fee of $79 for this service. http://www.how2findajob.com.

ResumeRabbit.com, Enter your resume on this site, and the site posts your resume to multiple major job sites. There is a fee of $59.95 for this service. http://start.resumerabbit.com

An Interview with Chris Strecker

A Multimedia Developer Specializing in Web, cdrom,

kiosk, 3D, and presentations. His take on the online job

search and how potential employees can make a

difference to him.

Employers often receive literally receive hundreds of responses to a job ad. How can applicants make sure their resume is read and portfolio viewed?

I look for a resume package that is clearly labeled and easy to read quickly with their strongest skillsets highlighted at the top.

More companies are using decision support systems that administer questionnaires online or at a kiosk in the personnel office, combine the answers with a digital resume, and make a decision based on preset parameters. How do job applicants benefit from this system and how does an artist showcase samples of his/her creative portfolio in this environment?

An applicant can best take advantage of this system by providing a link to an online portfolio of work.

Networking is about establishing informal relationships with other people, people who can provide information that can help in the job search. How does one find out about these networking meetings and how can applicants use networking to find the right job without being too pushy?

Look for local periodicals that publish weekly or monthly scheduled events in the creative industry, whether it be a showing at an art gallery or some social event at a local restaurant or bar. Something to meet local people face to face in the industry or nearly related industry.

What are the benefits/drawbacks to including temp work or an internships on your resume?

No drawback really. I like to know the full history of a potential employee. We more often than not look at creative individuals for freelance or project based rather than full-time.

How can a recruiter help applicants that have little or no job experience, and what should their first step be?

If an applicant has little real-world experience, focus on skills and get detailed about what they do the best or would like to be doing.

Should an applicant follow up the resume with a 'did you get it' phone call or what should their next step be after sending their resume?

A follow up phone call shows enthusiasm, but there is a fine line between enthusiastic and annoying. If most businesses are anything like ours, schedules are tight and time is valuable and scarce. The time it takes in dealing with lots of applicants can get out of hand easily.

Today's arts and technology company's dress code is often semiformal. For the initial job interview should one dress formally, and what are some things they can do to prepare for the interview?

No need for formal wear, but a well groomed neat appearance shows attention to detail and reflects heavily on who you are. A disheveled appearance is a red flag in my book. If they are sloppy in how they take care of themselves, it is almost a guarantee that they are going to be sloppy with their work.

What are some of the things one should never say or do during a job interview?

Don't use language similar to: "I don't really care"; "whatever"; "that's fine I guess." Apathy, doesn't sit well with me.

What kinds of advantages do students finishing schools now have over those that entered the job market say ten years ago?

They have the advantage of already knowing the latest software applications and their quicks and bugs, but someone in the same industry that entered the market ten years ago better stay on top of that kind of stuff anyway.

Chris Strecker
Multimedia Developer Specializing in Web, cdrom, kiosk, 3D, and presentations.

Rhubarb Productions
Orlando, Florida
(407) 895-5605

Email: chris@rhubarbproductions.com
http://www.rhubarbproductions.com

Resume Do's and Don'ts

The resume is the most important impression you will make on potential employers. It's your way in the door, but it can also be your way out. Check this list of Dos and Don'ts each and every time you prepare a resume to send out. If you are stuck on how to custom-tailor your resume, at the very least create one resume organized around your work experience and another organized around your different on-the-job skills. Depending on how many different types of skills you have, you may want to have a few versions of a skills-grouped resume: one that focuses on your fine art skills, and another that highlights your Web-specific design, and animation work, etc. With that said, here are those tips you need to keep in mind.

DO invest in a personal Web site. Spending $20 per month on a personal site allows you to build a product that showcases your skills and convinces future employers that you know what you are doing.

DO test your resume extensively and make sure it makes sense on all browsers and software.

DO include specific URLs of Web sites you have worked on, and list exactly what you did on the site or links to where any of your work can be seen online. And be sure to tell them exactly what you did and how you did it. Be specific. Being general won't impress anyone. But DON'T list too many URLs. Sometimes less is more.

If your specialty is interface design or computer graphics, DO include a click-through portfolio to showcase your knowledge and experience.

DO offer a printable version of your online resume. If someone is looking to recruit you, he or she will want a hard copy for interviews.

DO practice good resume writing skills. Observe the same rules of writing for all versions of your resume.

Using Resume Keywords

Keywords are the nouns and noun phrases used by recruiters and employers searching through applicant databases and Web job sites for resumes for potential candidates. Keywords are a relatively new requirement. This requirement developed when employers and agencies began storing resumes in applicant databases. When the Internet became the main means of looking for a job, keywords became important. You will want to keep them in mind when designing your resume and looking for a position online.

First of all, job candidates need to think of the education and experience they have had and the job they want. Start by brainstorming a list of nouns and verbs on a piece of paper that would describe you, your previous positions, and the position you hope to get. If you can, get a copy of the job description for the job you want, and pick out the noun and noun phrases used.

Developing Your Keywords

You will want to be creative when coming up with keywords, but don't be inaccurate. Make a list of the following:

· Standard job titles, particularly if current or former employers used non-standard titles.

· Names of job-specific, profession-specific, and industry-specific tools that you use or are qualified to use because of education and/or experience.

· Software and hardware that you use or have been trained to use, particularly if it's unique to your job, industry, or profession.

· Names of techniques that you use or are qualified to use.

· Industry and professional organizations that you have joined.

· Professional and/or technical acronyms. Again, it's important to be accurate here.

· Applicable education that you have, including degrees and specific courses that are relevant to your career.

· Other jargon that describes your work, typical products, and/or services involved, and the people who do your job. This may be specific computer-graphic or animation terms.

Adding Keywords to Your Resume

In the main body of your resume, include the acronyms and keywords that you came up with. Use it in conjunction with your job descriptions and in other areas of your resume. This will increase the probability that your resume will appear in an employer or recruiter's search results.

Be inconsistent. Believe it or not, this is an advantage in the resume search-ability game. Don't destroy your resume, but be as creative as you can when using your keywords. Try using "M.B.A," "MBA," "Master of Business Administration," "Masters in Bus. Admin," etc. so your resume will pop up in the results regardless of the exact term used in the search.

Add a section near the top of your resume named "skills" or "keywords," where you concentrate as many of your keywords as possible. Using a "Skills Summary" is a great way to make your resume stand out as well as come up in the search engines. Use the nouns and noun phrases that best summarize the experience and skills as well as education and relevant association memberships.

The Regional Online Job Search

If you are looking for a job in a specific region, you may want to consider using regional job sites as well as the more general career sites like careerpath.com. Job seekers may even find that some of the better positions aren't listed on the big sites but instead listed with local papers and other smaller advertisers. It's worth your time to look into the regional sites. The number of newspapers with an online presence continues to grow. Here are a few to get you started.

For the South Try: The News & Observer Triangle.com Section

http://www.newsobserver.com/classified/jobs/index.html

Raleigh-Durham's The News & Observer has grown from a local newspaper site into a national portal for news and employment. There are several positions available in the arts and many are well-paid.

For the East try: The Boston Globe Boston Work Section

http://careers.boston.com/

The Boston Globe's career section is filled for people looking for art-related jobs. You will have to use specific keywords to search, but the jobs are there.

For the Midwest try: The Minneapolis Star-Tribune Work Avenue Section

http://www.startribune.com/workavenue/

The Minneapolis Star-Tribune is a good online job source for people looking for employment in the Chicago area. If you live anywhere around Minnesota, this site provides fresh job listings for the Midwest.

For the West try: The Portland Oregonian Advance Careers Section

http://www.oregonlive.com/advancecareers/

The Portland Oregonian's employment section has not only recent and well-organized listings, it's also one of the few newspapers with a job search function for computers and art that even offers dozens of subcategories.

The New Era of Job-Seeking: Strategies for Finding Employment on the Internet

The Web presents the job seekers of today with some great new avenues for finding new employment. But like anything, you have got to do it with a little strategy in mind. Successfully navigating this frontier requires new skills and strategies.

The Web presents a whole plethora of job seeking resources. From employment sites, to career advice, to recruiters, to companies that only advertise their jobs online the choices can be a bit overwhelming. Where to start, how can you make yourself stand out, what's going to get you the job? While looking for a job on the Internet should be your first choice in today's world, it should by no means be the only job-seeking strategy you use. The traditional methods of networking, job boards, classified ads, and targeted job searches should still be part of your overall job-seeking plan. The Internet simply expands the job-seeking resources that are available to you.

You can begin the job search by going to some of the larger career sites like careerpath.com or flipdog.com. These sites can get you started by offering you assistance with developing or honing your resume and cover letter writing, finding the best sources for researching companies, strengthening your interviewing skills, learning how to network, mastering salary negotiation, as well as perfecting other key career and job-seeking skills. If you only have one type of resume, then you should definitely start here. Today, there are three common types of resumes:

The traditional resume is your basic version with formatting and plenty of accomplishments listed and lots of actions verbs.

The scannable resume is a stripped down version of your traditional resume, in plain text for easy scanning into computer databases.

The Web-based resume is similar to your traditional resume, but published on your personal Web site so that is always available to potential employers.

Once you figure out what kind of resume you'll need and how you'll lay it out, you'll need to start thinking about what you'll do with these fancy resumes of yours. There are four different types of Web resources for job seekers:

Networking Sites and Discussion Lists: There are thousands of Internet-based discussion lists on almost every subject and profession imaginable. Join one or more of these lists and network with people in your field; employers sometimes subscribe to these lists to screen potential candidates.

Resume Sites and Job Banks: Web sites such as HotJobs, FlipDog.com, and CareerMosaic have large databases of job openings where candidates can search by profession or keywords. Many of these sites allow users to post a resume for free, and some even offer job and applicant matching services.

Specialized Job Sites: There are also hundreds of specialized job Web sites, from employment recruiters of all types to specialized job databank sites that focus on a specific industry including the arts. A list of the best of these specialized job sites can be found at Quintessential Careers: Career and Job-Seeking Resources by Industry at http://www.quintcareers.com/indres.html.

Company Web sites. If you have a specific set of companies you would most like to work for, the best solution might simply be to go the each company's Web site and review job postings. Many of these companies allow you to apply online, and they often list the contact person so you should be able to easily follow-up, as you would if you sent a cover letter and resume to an employer. Plus, many of the positions you will find on the site won't be advertised on any of the job sites. Remember to keep this in mind when looking for a specific type of position.

None of these sites or strategies will guarantee that you will find the exact job you are looking for, but they are certainly your best defense against unemployment. Remember not to just use one strategy but use them all with each other.

45 Ways to Ace Your Interview

The best defense you'll have when sitting in the interview chair is being prepared. The following are a list of questions and suggestions to keep in mind before the big day arrives. Be prepared, be calm and confident, and you'll score big.

General Questions

1. Tell me about yourself.

·   Keep your answer to one or two minutes. Don't ramble.

·   If you have a profile or personal statement at the top of your CV use this as your starting point.

2. What do you know about our company?

·   Research the company's products, size, reputation, image, goals, problems, management style, people, skills, history and philosophy.

·   Be informed and interested. Let the interviewer tell you about the company, let them define their business in their terms.

3. Why do you want to work for us?

·   Don't talk about what you want; first talk about their needs.

- You want to be part of an exciting forward-moving company.

- You can make a definite contribution to specific company goals.

4. What would you do for us? What can you do for us that someone else can't?

- Relate past experiences that represent success in working for your previous employer.

- Talk about your fresh perspective and the relevant experience you can bring to the company.

- Highlight your track record of providing creative, workable solutions.

5. What do you find the most attractive about this position? Least attractive?

- List a couple of attractive factors such as the responsibility the post offers and the opportunity to work with experienced teams that have a reputation for innovation and creativity.

- Say you'd need more information and time before being able to make a judgment on any unattractive aspects.

6. Why should we hire you?

- Because of knowledge, experience, abilities, and skills.

7. What do you look for in a job?

- An opportunity to use skills, to perform and be recognized.

8. Please give me your definition of a ... (the position for which you are being interviewed).

· Keep it brief and actions/results-oriented.

9. How long would it take you to make a meaningful contribution to our firm?

· Very quickly – after a couple of weeks getting to know your system and clients and a brief period of adjustment on the learning curve.

· Highlight that you're a quick learner and used to adapting to new situations.

10. How long would you stay with us?

· As long as we both feel I'm contributing, achieving, growing etc.

Job Search Questions

11. Why are you leaving your present job?

· Try to give positive reasons.

· Give a 'group' answer if possible, such as your department was consolidated or eliminated.

12. Why haven't you found a new position before now?

· Finding a job is easy but finding the right job is more difficult. Make it sound like you're being 'selective'.

13. Had you thought of leaving your present position before? If yes, what do you think held you there?

· Challenge, but it's gone now.

14. What other types of jobs or companies are you considering?

· Keep your answer related to this company's field. You want to sound focused.

15. Describe what you feel to be an ideal working environment.

· Where people are treated as fairly as possible.

16. How would you evaluate your present firm?

· An excellent company which afforded me many fine experiences.

17. What do you think of your current boss?

· Be as positive as you can and explain working with him/her was a learning experience.

Your Work Habits

18. If I spoke with your previous boss, what would he say are your greatest strengths and weaknesses?

· Emphasize skills—don't be too negative about your weaknesses; it's always safe to identify a lack of a skill or experience as a shortcoming rather than a personal characteristic.

19. Can you work under pressure and to deadline?

· Yes. Quite simply, it is a way of life in business.

20. How have you changed the nature of your job?

· Improved it…of course.

21. In your present position, what problems have you identified that had previously been overlooked?

· Keep it brief and don't brag.

22. Don't you feel you might be better off in a smaller/larger company? Different type of company?

· Depends on the job—elaborate slightly.

23. How do you resolve conflict on a project team?

· First discuss issues privately.

24. What was the most difficult decision you ever had to make?

· Attempt to relate your response to the prospective employment situation.

Experience and Management Questions

25. You may be overqualified or too experienced for the position we have to offer.

· Strong companies need strong people.

· Experienced executives are in great demand today.

· Emphasize your interest in making a long-term commitment.

· The employer will get a faster return on investment because you have more experience than required.

· A growing, energetic company is rarely unable to use its people's talents.

26. What is your management style?

- If you've never thought about this, it's high time you did.
- Open door is best, but you get the job done on time or inform your manager.

27. Are you a good manager? Give an example.

- Keep your answer achievement- and task-oriented
- Emphasize your management prowess: planning, organizing, and communication skills.

28. What do you look for when you hire people?

- Skills, initiative, adaptability.

29. Have you ever fired anyone? If so, what were the reasons and how did you handle it?

- Explain your experience of this and how you overcame any problems.

30. What do you see as the most difficult task in being a manager?

- Focus on the bigger picture—getting things planned and done on time within the budget.

31. What do your subordinates think of you?

- Be honest and positive, they can probably check up if they choose to.

32. What is your biggest weakness as a manager?

- Be honest and end on a positive note, for example, "I have a problem reprimanding people so I always begin with something positive first."

Quantifying Your Experience and Accomplishments

33. Have you helped increase sales? Profits? How?

· Describe your contribution in some detail.

34. Have you helped reduce costs? How?

· Describe your contribution in some detail.

35. How much money did you ever account for?

· Be specific.

36. How many people did you supervise on your last job?

· Be specific.

37. In your current or last position, what features did you like the most? Least?

· Be honest but positive.

38. In your current or last position, what are or were your five most significant accomplishments?

· Refer to the key accomplishments already identified on your CV.

Salary Questions

39. How much are you looking for?

· Answer with a question, i.e., "What is the salary range for similar jobs in your company?"

· If they don't answer, then give a range of what you understand you are worth to be in the marketplace.

40. How much would you expect, if we offer you this position?

·   Be careful; the market value of the job may be the key answer. Say something like: "My understanding is that a job like the one you're describing may be in the range of…"

41. What kind of salary are you worth?

·   Have a specific figure in mind and don't be hesitant.

Personality Questions

42. What are your interests?

·   Show that you lead a balanced life. For example talk about books, films and activities you do outside work.

43. How would you describe your own personality?

·   Balanced.

44. What are your strong points?

·   Present at least three and relate them to the interviewing company and job opening.

45. What are your weak points?

·   Don't say you have none.

·   Try not to cite personal characteristics as weaknesses, but be ready to have one if interviewer presses.

·   Turn a negative into a positive answer: "I am sometimes intent on completing an assignment and get too deeply involved when we are late."

Get the Right Job the First Time

Getting a job for the first time or after a long break can be a daunting prospect. It certainly gets better with practice, but is rarely an activity that comes easily or naturally to most people. You are bound to feel exposed, judged, and extremely vulnerable. It's normal. So what can you do? How about finding the right job the first time you look? That's the only sure-fire way to make sure you don't have go on another intimidating interview again.

The Blanks

The initial stumbling block for first-timers is having no track record. Faced with a blank application form, the spaces for experience can look very large without anything to fill them in with.

If you have the choice, apply using a CV and cover letter. You can do more justice to yourself at this stage by concentrating on transferable skills and demonstrating how they can be applied to the job you are targeting.

If you have to use a conventional form there's nothing to stop you using the space differently. Write a note in the experience sections explaining that this is an application for your first job, directing the reader to additional information you have enclosed that demonstrates your suitability for the job. It will show that you approach problems creatively.

Believing in Yourself

Lack of self-confidence afflicts newcomers to the world of work and those returning after a break. It's easy to feel at a disadvantage when some of the terms used mean nothing to you or if you are worried that you haven't kept up with the latest technologies.

From the outside it can look as if everyone knows what they're doing and that what they're involved in is complicated and difficult to master. Once you get into an organization you soon realize it's staffed by ordinary people doing things that are easy to learn.

If It Doesn't Work Out

If your first job is not your ideal, see it as a training ground for better things to come. Just having a job makes you more confident about looking for other jobs. However, don't make the mistake of taking the first thing that comes along just to prove that someone wants you. If this experience is a bad one the negative effects can cause ripples for a long time.

Jobs that don't work out should be treated as valuable learning experiences. The early phases of a career are an experimental stage in life. You do not know whether a job that involves shift work, lots of travel, or mainly working on your own is right for you until you've tried it. Finding what does and doesn't suit you eliminates possibilities and brings you closer to finding the perfect job.

Online Job Applications

More and more companies are using online job applications to seek out qualified job candidates. Not only does it prove that the applicant is computer literate, but it's a fast and effective means of getting to know a candidate. Most employers now offer online options to applicants. These include:

·   application forms that are completed and sent via the Web,

·   forms that can be downloaded from the Web but need to be printed and returned by mail,

·   requests for resumes with cover letters to be sent as emails.

The focus of online job applications is obviously the content. Electronic applications don't have the distractions of messy handwriting and crumpled paper so they often make things less complicated for the employer.

Online Forms

Online forms can be found on almost every Web site around on the Internet anymore. They are especially popular in the career section of corporate Web sites both for current vacancies and to attract speculative applicants. But there are a few things job seekers should keep in mind before succumbing to these tempting online forms. Don't be tempted to complete and submit an online form immediately. Take the same time and care as you would over a paper application form. Either print off the form and work on a hard copy first or copy and paste it into a word processing package. Many forms have both optional and compulsory fields. Always complete sections that ask for more detailed background information. They give employers an insight into what's special about you. When pasting from a word processing package to an online form don't rely on the spellchecker. Do a visual check too. Print the online form and read it carefully before submitting. Remember to save a copy of the completed form for yourself.

Downloadable Forms

Some employers offer their forms as downloads you can save to disk. The two most common formats are PDF or DOC files. The most common downloadable forms are in PDF which requires Adobe Acrobat Reader. Most sites which provide documents in this format incorporate a link to an Adobe download page. Although you can look at and print a PDF file, you will not be able to fill it in using your computer. You need to print the form, complete it by hand, then post it using conventional mail. Most employer sites will let you know which way they'd prefer to receive it back.

Emailed Resumes

Employers who ask for applications by email are expecting at least a resume. Some want to receive a cover letters; others say specifically not to include it. As a rule, never give them more than what they ask for. Employers will also make it clear as to whether your resume should be sent as an attachment or as plain text within the body of an email. If you are not sure, check with them. Recent problems with viruses in mail attachments have made companies wary. Many automatically delete unsolicited mail with attachments without looking at it. Again, always give them what they ask for. As for emailed resumes, here are a few other things to keep in mind:

- Remember your mail reader may not be the same as an employer's so the simpler you keep things the more likely it is to look good. More isn't always better. Just because it looks one way on your screen, doesn't mean that it will end up on the other end that way. Avoid using email formatting tools and just keep your resume simple.

- You can compose your resume in Word or another word processing program and then cut and paste into an email. Check appearance and spacing and edit as necessary.

- Always complete the subject line. Make it clear and concise, the name of the job you are applying for and its reference number works well.

- Start with a career summary or employment objective, put contact details at the end. Your name and email address appear at the top of a message automatically.

- See what your resume looks like by opening it in your outbox or sending it to yourself.

Finding a Good Employment Agency

You will find a lot of employment agencies and recruiters along the road to finding the perfect job. Employment agencies can be valuable allies but not all of them are measured the same. There are several different agency types and you should know exactly what they do in order to find the one that best suits you and your career needs.

Temporary Services: These agencies deal specifically with providing businesses with temporary help. Those businesses pay the temporary agency which, in turn, pays the employee.

Private Placement Firms: These companies basically match employees to employers. The placement service will charge a fee, but usually only when someone is actually hired. It is typically the employer who pays the fee, but this depends upon the individual placement firm.

Retained Search Firms: Companies hire these firms to find workers—usually at the executive level. The company looking for workers pays their fee, which isn't dependent upon whether or not anyone is actually hired.

Job Listing Services: These companies are different from actual employment agencies in that they don't actually place anyone in jobs. Rather, they collect information on jobs that are out there and sell consolidated lists.

Executive Counseling Services: These companies help you to write effective resumes, make good career decisions, and improve interviewing abilities. They don't actually help you find jobs or place you anywhere. They just help you know what to do when you find one of your own. They charge you a fee regardless of whether or not you find a job.

Public Employment Services: This service is provided by the government at no cost and often has resources available such as career counseling and job screening. They can also refer you to an appropriate job training service. They will help job seekers with preparing a resume, interviewing skills, and evaluating skills. They provide particular support to senior citizens, the disabled, veterans, and public aid recipients.

Mastering the Online Interview

The online interview is designed to save time. It allows employers to know the ins and outs of a job applicant before you even walk into the door. For example, Net-Interview, offered by Advantage Hiring, is an electronic screening tool that becomes part of an electronic job posting. Candidates' answers are automatically stored in a database, scored and ranked, and compared the requirements the hiring manager has established. The hiring manager is presented with a "short list" of candidates based on the electronic prescreening, and is given a customized list of questions to against ask each candidate. That short list would otherwise take days to compile—the ability to generate it automatically can be a big time-saver for shops that may receive hundreds or even thousands of resumes a week.

Unicru's Smart Assessment technology also applies decision support to find patterns in a company's employment history data and apply that knowledge to the selection process. Like Net Interview, Smart Assessment generates a customized list of interview questions and creates a short list of qualified candidates for the hiring manager.

With the online interview, you will need at least 45 minutes to answer a slew of questions such as:

- Would you rather have structure or flexibility in your job?

- How often do you forget important details?

- How often do your decisions have unexpected consequences?

- In the past, what approach have you chosen for solving difficult problems?

- How would you react to working without direct supervision, setting your own goals, and meeting them?

- In what type of work environment are you most productive?

- In the past, when you were assigned numerous tasks with little direction, how did you react?

These questions are done completely online, but don't let the informality fool you. Answer these questions wrong and you will never get a face-to-face interview, much less a phone call. But determining "wrong" and "right" answers is not so simple. The answer you may think they want to hear may not be the right one after all. How do you ace these tricky assessment interviews? It is done not by telling companies what they want to hear, but by simply being honest. How would you answer questions like, "In the past, what approach have you taken to solving difficult problems?"

1. I have thoroughly investigated all aspects of the job.

2. I have felt overwhelmed and asked someone for help.

3. I have requested guidance from my supervisor or professor to find the solution.

4. I have given up and moved on to a new task.

5. I don't know.

Or:

How do you feel about making unpopular decisions?

1. I like to make decisions I know will be unpopular.

2. I have no problem making unpopular decisions.

3. I don't like to make unpopular decisions, but I can if necessary.

4. I prefer not to make unpopular decisions.

5. I can't make unpopular decisions.

6. I have never made an unpopular decision.

I bet you'd pick No. 1 for the first question and No. 2 for the second. But, you could be making a big mistake. Why? Because companies want to hear from people who want to get along with other people. They don't want candidates who can guess the right answer on a test. The obvious answer to the second question is 3—no one wants to be unpopular so it's the "honest" answer. In the first question, the job may not require someone who stays with a problem until doomsday, but someone who asks for help and moves to the next problem. This means they're looking for someone with a particular personality trait. In this case, there's no "right" answer.

The bottom line is this: If you are faced with taking one of the online questionnaires, don't sweat it. There's just no way to fail at it. If you don't hear from the employer, it's probably not a good match anyway. Remember, the most popular answer isn't necessarily "your" answer.

Getting the Most Out of a Job Fair

Going to a job fair and figuring out how to navigate through dozens or hundreds of exhibition tables filled with potential employers isn't as hard as it seems. It's a chance for job seekers to shine again and again. But it's not just about looking for job openings. There are other benefits: researching companies, identifying who's hiring, practicing interviewing skills, and practicing networking skills. But as with anything, a little preparation will take you a long way. The following are a few things you should do before heading out the convention center:

Invest in a business card so that you have something to hand out to company representatives.

Develop and refine your resume and bring plenty of clean copies. You will need them.

Identify at least 20 companies you wish to target. It's wise to go through the listing of companies that will be represented at the fair; it will help you select companies that you will then be able to research beforehand.

Create a 60-second introduction that summarizes your experience, skills, personal traits, why you are looking for a new position, and what position you are seeking. Memorize it. You only have one first impression so do it right each time.

Prepare a list of questions for the companies. You need to know more about the company: You're buying, they're buying; you're selling, they're selling.

Have a positive outlook. Approach the fair with enthusiasm and confidence and have fun. Every one of those places is an opportunity. You are going there to collect information and make connections, as well as to practice your job-search skills.

Getting the Most Out of the Experience

Don't rush through the fair. Set aside more than an hour or two to spend there. You will need more time than that to make your way through it comfortably. Plan to be there for a day or two half-days. There's just so much opportunity there. It may help to take someone with you. Perhaps a friend that's also job seeking, a colleague, or someone else that would get something out of the experience.

Ideally, you want to hand out a copy of your resume and talk to someone at the table, to each company there. To get the most out of a job fair, this should be your plan. You never know what you'll learn at each table, even if you aren't necessarily looking for a job with each company.

And by all means, dress appropriately. Treat a job fair as a potential interview because that's exactly what it will be. Each time you stop a table you may or may not land a job. Be prepared to stand in line to talk to company representatives. You can make use of that time to talk to people around you. You may want to hand out your business card to them and collect theirs. You want to collect company information from the tables. Anything they have—brochures, annual reports, or business cards. They may come in handy later.

When you approach a company representative, smile, shake hands firmly, and be prepared to launch into your 60-second introduction. And know what you want to ask a particular company before you show up at their table. Give it some thought before you approach a rep from the company. Be prepared with questions to ask them about their company and be prepared for a screening interview. Although few people actually get hired at a job fair, you need to be prepared for an interview on the spot. And finally, thank each person that you meet for their time.

Following Up

You do need to follow up with companies of interest and especially companies with which you have had a screening. Sort through the information you have collected, and take the next step with each company of interest. If they suggested you call, do just that. If they suggested you email, be sure to drop them a line. These contacts are valuable and you don't want to lose a good thing.

5 Things to Take Away From a Career Fair

1. Business cards from the recruiters you have met. Use the cards to write follow-up notes to those organizations in which you are most interested.

2. Notes about contacts you made. Take paper and pen with you to write down important details about particular organizations, including names of people who may not have had business cards. Take a few minutes after you leave each table to jot down these notes.

3. Information about organizations you have contacted. Most recruiters will have information for you to pick up, including company brochures, computer disks, or CD's, position descriptions, and other data.

4. A better sense of your career options. If you have used the event correctly, you will have made contact with several organizations that hire people with your skills and interests. In thinking about their needs and your background, evaluate whether each company might be a match for you.

5. Self-confidence in interacting with employer representatives. A career fair gives you the opportunity to practice your interview skills in a less formidable environment than a formal interview. Use this experience to

practice talking about what you have done, what you know, and what your interests are.

Sample
Thank You Letter

Conservative/ Formal

John Charles
838 Marian Way
Herndon, VA 27599
(919) 555-1212

Dr. Joan Nagle
Technical Design Group Director
Casey Design Systems Inc.
81796 Gulick Road
Charlotte, NC 28235

Dear Dr. Nagle:

I want to thank you very much for interviewing me yesterday for the graphic design position. I enjoyed meeting you and learning more about your research and design work.

The interview strengthened my enthusiasm for the position and interest in working for Casey. I believe my education and cooperative education experiences fit nicely with the job requirements, and I'm certain I could make a significant contribution to the firm over time.

I would like to reiterate my strong interest in the position and in working with you and your staff. You provide the kind of opportunity I seek. Please feel free to call me at the telephone number listed above if I can provide you with any additional information.

Again, thank you for the interview and for your consideration.

Sincerely,

John Charles

Understanding the Want Ads

If you have ever perused the want ads on or offline, you have probably learned one thing: You have got to know how to read between the lines to know what employers are really looking for. Reading the want ads and understanding them is an art, and mastering it can keep you from wasting potential employers' time and your own.

Education

Ultimately, employers want the best person for the job. Employers soliciting for a B.S. or M.S. in some area of the arts would be very pleased if such a person applied. More important than a degree, however, is the capability to perform. If you don't have the exact education, don't immediately cross the ad off your list. You may still have a chance to get in. But you need to do it cleverly. If you know you don't have the required education, you will need to approach things differently. If they asked for a Bachelor's and you don't have one, think about what you do have and what makes you qualified in spite of your lack of education. If you have years of experience in the field, be proud and don't be shy about boasting. In fact, it should be the very first thing you mention. Put that right in the cover letter so they see it right away. Don't let them skip right past you because of your education. Try something like this as an opener: "I suspect that it's going to be tempting to throw out this resume because I don't have a bachelor's degree. I made a conscious choice to do my learning in the real world. I've done things that I never could have done if I had been sitting in a class. I'm a go-getter, but now we've reached the moment of truth. Will you interview me?" How could they turn you down?

Experience

Experience is measured in years. But quality always comes before quantity. In the want ads, you are bound to see some arbitrary requirements. Some employers want to see five years of experience no matter what you've done. Others want only two years of solid, hard experience. But again, it's almost always about quality over quantity. Keep this in mind when you're presenting yourself. Don't be shy about what you've been doing. Bring your experience to life with an anecdote or two explaining an employment-related problem you faced and how you resolved it.

Hard Skills

If it's a technical position and they have got skill and competency requirements, you can't fake that. If they ask for very specific skills, such as software or programming skills, you need to have the skills. Placing a want ad is expensive; if a company spends valuable space describing specific skills, you had better have at least some of them. Weakness in one area is acceptable, but basic knowledge is expected. Most experts say that strength in two out of three is reasonable. If you are only lacking one hard skill, you can still apply; just highlight what you do know.

Soft Skills

Soft skills are a little bit more negotiable. Extracting the kind of values and work ethic a company espouses by the soft skills that it stresses in its ad, such as travel and a desire to learn, can help you decide if you want to apply. Soft skills are those that run in the gray area. Soft skills such as leadership, project, and management skills are a sign that the company doesn't want a person to come in and learn things one by one, but wants someone who's not afraid of a challenge. Someone that will come in and get things done.

Are All Ads Real?

You would think that if an employer takes the time to place a want ad, that there's an actual position that they're trying to fill. But that's not always the case. Some companies use ads as a kind of public relations stunt to showcase themselves as up-and-coming. Some larger companies have an ongoing need for employees and use the ads to generate resumes for unspecified future positions. Many organizations that receive federal funds are required by law to place ads, even if there is an internal candidate ready to take the position. An ad that is extraordinarily specific should also raise a red flag; employers know that nobody could possibly fit the qualifications and probably have an insider in mind.

Working with Recruiters

Recruiters are an increasingly important part of many professionals' job searches, and job seekers will find them everywhere on the Web. Recruiters are especially abundant the IT professions where the jobs are abundant. But some people get called by recruiters and others simply don't. So what's the difference? How can you get a recruiter to help you find a decent job? How can you weed through the bad ones? The following paragraphs will help you to understand the tactics of recruiters and how you can get them to work for you.

To understand why some people get called by recruiters and others don't it helps to first look at how recruiters operate. The main thing to remember is that recruiters work for the companies whose positions they are trying to fill, not for the job seeker. Some recruiters, especially those who fill staff and midlevel management positions, work on contingency, which means they are paid only if they fill a position. In some cases more than one contingency recruiter may be trying to fill a job. Other recruiters work on retainer, which means they get paid for doing a search, regardless of the outcome. This kind of recruiter is typically used to find senior managers and executives. Some recruiters do both kinds of searches, depending on the position, but most specialize in one type or the other.

Because retained recruiters are paid for the search, they are likely to be more concerned about whether they are finding the right person for the job. If they do place you, it's more likely to be a good match, but they may not be as likely to find a job for you.

Both types of recruiters are typically looking for candidates who can fill immediate openings and for people to keep on their lists to match future positions. One consequence of the tight labor market, however, is that many recruiters are working harder to fill current openings and so have less time to spend developing contacts with candidates for future positions.

None of this means that recruiters are bad, or that job seekers should avoid working with them. The best recruiters try to place the right candidates in the right jobs even when they are working on contingency, because if they place good candidates, companies will give them new assignments. A good relationship with a good recruiter can be an invaluable career tool.

If you are not getting a lot of calls from recruiters, don't worry about it. Instead of focusing on the number of calls you are getting, work on establishing long-term relationships with good recruiters. The job search process is not quick one. Things take time. Just because a recruiter doesn't have something this week, doesn't mean that he or she won't the next.

Resume Traps

The worst thing any job seeker can do on a resume is lie. Even when your experience or education is lacking, you don't want to be dishonest about your education or job history. While it may help you in the short-term, it's not going to get you anywhere in the long-run and someone is going to find the loophole. But what about when you're not lying? When a potential employer starts checking the facts on your resume, even areas where you told the truth can raise red flags. There are three resume pitfalls that can cause an employer to question your integrity. Knowing about them ahead of time, will give you time to prepare a response to any questions a potential employer may have.

Changing Company Names

If a former employer has changed names, been bought out, or moved, do yourself and your potential employer a favor and note the new name or location on your resume. This way, when the resume checkers can't find your former employer in its former city, they won't have to do a lot of detective work to verify your employment.

Contract Positions

If you worked on a long-term project for a company, by all means list it on your resume. But if your paycheck was actually coming from a consulting or staffing company, specify that as well. Otherwise, when resume checkers call the company you list, they will be told you were never on the payroll.

Inaccurate Job Titles

Be as accurate as possible when listing actual job titles. If the titles on your resume don't match what the companies tell the employer that it may cause concern. It's better to not list a title at all than to give one that's inaccurate.

Being up front about any questionable items on your resume is only going to help you. Anything you can do to show that you're willing to make your employer's job easier is going to win you points. Always be honest up front.

Choosing Between Two Job Offers

It doesn't happen too often, but it happens. How do you decide between two job offers? You know it's a crossroads that could ultimately change your life for the good or bad, but how do you decide the right choice? Although many people would be delighted to have just one good offer, choosing between two offers can be stressful.

Job Satisfaction

The quality of your work and personal life will greatly influence your job satisfaction. Take this into consideration when evaluating a job offer. Take a real, hard look at what they have to offer as a community, as a culture. You will be spending lots of time there. Ask yourself questions such as:

- Do I feel comfortable with my supervisor and the people I have met?

- Is a formal training program or on-the-job training—where risk and responsibility come fairly quickly—a better fit for me?

- Typically, what happens to people after their first or second year in the job?

- Are my job responsibilities too narrow, or do they build upon the future?

· Where are other branches of the organization and when can I relocate?

Salary Package

When evaluating a salary offer or choosing between offers, look at the whole entire package, not just at the salary. Benefits, such as health insurance, retirement contribution, and tuition reimbursement for graduate studies, can equal 25%-40% of the total salary package. Use the following information to evaluate a salary package:

· Written description of responsibilities.

· Start date.

· Starting salary, including benefits package.

· Comparative salary and cost of living information.

· Vacation time.

· Salary review schedule. When will your first performance review and possible salary increase occur?

· Signing bonus—is one offered?

· Relocation stipend—are moving expenses or trips to locate housing included?

· Stock options, if applicable.

Other Factors to Consider

· Company reputation and financial stability.

· Job security.

- Facilities and working conditions.

- Size of company.

- Type of industry.

- Sector of the economy—public, private, or non-profit?

- Amount of travel required.

- Training programs and educational opportunities.

- Advancement opportunities.

- Geographic location, cost of living, and relocation expense.

Negotiating a Salary Package

Just about all job offers are negotiable, even the salary. You don't have to take the first offer they give you, but you do have to be willing to speak up and ask for more. It is not impolite or unprofessional to negotiate. If the salary is fair, you may prefer to negotiate on other issues, such as a signing bonus. When negotiating, use your facts, not your feelings. Don't say, "I feel that I am more qualified than the average candidate." Instead, say something a little more significant such as, "I have had three internships in the field and will have a shorter learning curve." To negotiate, you will need to offer a salary range based on how your industry rates in the national salary surveys. Be prepared to accept the low end of the range you suggest. Salary calculators, cost of living, and relocation expense estimates can be found on Web sites such as http://www.homefair.com/home/ and http://www.accra.org/.

Delaying Your Response

If you need time to think about your offers, you will need to let the employer know. It's common courtesy to let them know that you're thinking about it. After all, if you are not going go take the job, they will have to find someone else. If you have more second interviews scheduled or need more time to consider the decision or explore other possibilities, contact the employer and let them know. Usually a phone call or short letter will suffice.

Accepting an Offer

When you are ready to accept an offer, call or write and express your appreciation for the offer and state that you are looking forward to joining the organization. If applicable, specify when you will meet additional conditions of employment, such as a completing a medical exam or sending required documents.

Declining an Offer

Verbally decline the offer, and then send a well-written letter thanking the employer for their efforts in recruiting you and for the offer. Explain why the offer you are taking better matches your needs or desires at this point in time. Keep the door open for future associations with the firm by expressing your appreciation of the opportunity to interview. Re-entering the Workforce

Finding a job is rarely easy, and job seekers trying to return to the workforce after years away from it face extra challenges. The challenges of re-entering the job market are enough to make some people question stepping out of it at all. It's not hard to get back in after a long break, especially in today's fast-changing, technological world. But looking for a job after taking time off is not all that different from looking for one when you are already working. You need to do all the things that beginners need to do. Figure where you want to work and what you want to do and then get those skills updated. And of course, network, network, and then network some more.

Before starting your job search, you really need to identify exactly what it is that you want to do. Just because your last job had you doing a certain thing in the arts, doesn't mean that that's what you want to do now. You need to take some time to re-evaluate yourself, your skills, and your position in life. Knowing exactly what you want will help you get exactly what you need. Once you know what kind of work you would like, you need to convince a company that you can make a significant contribution. In today's world, it's always a matter of "What can you do for me?" Every employer will want to know your answer to that question.

You will need to think about what contributions you have made to employers over the years. If you have been out of the workplace for a while, you will need to make sure your skills are up-to-date and you must convince employers that are comfortable with these skills and can get the job done. Most companies are looking for proof that you can apply your knowledge in a business setting.

It's especially important for candidates that are reentering the workforce to follow the steps of networking by remembering the following:

1. Know what you want. There are many people networking to get back in and their questions are so broad that nobody can help.

2. Know who's out there. Take a look at who is easy for you to call. Take a look at who is harder for you to call, and who knows who.

3. Know precisely the kind of help you want from others. Do you want someone just to connect you with other people? Do you want someone to sponsor you in some professional society or organization?

4. Know the odds. Networking to get back inside will take time, money, and energy.

5. Know what to offer. For everyone you ask something of, you should offer up something in return. There's an exchange of favors. You have to think in terms of what your own currencies are.

Networking is a valuable tool for anyone job searching, but it's especially helpful for job seekers that have been out of the loop for a while. Use every tool that you have and make your intentions clear. With the right combination of initiative, energy, and luck, reentering the workplace will be a breeze.

Will a New Job Help You Advance?

Knowing the right time to switch jobs will determine just how quickly you succeed in your career. Keep in mind that the pace of change within the area of technology is now so rapid that you may be able to learn a lot even if you stay with your current company. There are several things you need to keep in mind before deciding whether now is the right time to switch.

Advancement

If you are thinking of switching jobs because you want to advance in your career, make sure that taking a new position will do just that. You want to be sure your new employer offers room for advancement. If you are interested in management, find out whether the company has a history of promoting from within. Find out if the company is growing, has a history of expanding, or if it seems to be staying the same. There will always be more opportunities for growth in an expanding business.

If you aren't interested in advancing, look to see if the employer offers the opportunity for growth. You'll most certainly want to expand upon your skills and stay up-to-date with the changing world. Find out if the employer will back you on this. What type of training or workshops will they offer in the future?

Money

Don't let money be your main motivation for changing jobs, but think about it long and hard. Where do you want be financially in five years? Will this job help you get there? And don't forget stock options and benefits when you are playing the numbers game. It all adds up.

Other Factors to Consider

You want to be sure you are not going to inherit too many problems that others have left behind. Don't be shy about asking why the new position is open. Watch for the red flags in interviews. If the interviewer asks you if doing such-and-such will be a problem for you, that probably means the department has had trouble with it in the past. Really read between the lines. If an employer speaks badly about the person who previously held the position, there are big problems there. And you don't want to start a position with problems already in place. Of course, you take a certain risk when you switch companies, because the last hired can also be the first fired, but consider all the factors.

Why Create a Portfolio?

The traditional portfolio is used by artists, photographers, and graphic designers to demonstrate samples of their work. Unlike a cover letter, resume, or application form, a portfolio demonstrates how one's skills, experiences, and history match a position. A one page list of the "Portfolio Contents" sent with your cover letter and resume allows the employer to screen your qualifications quickly and then request items from your portfolio, if desired.

A portfolio is the central representation of what you as a designer, illustrator, or fine artist are capable of doing. Besides your resume, this is an essential tool for communication with potential employers. It's what's going to stand out most for you. It represents you as an artist, a person, and as a potential employee. The following outline details portfolio needs and the similarities and differences for different types of artists looking to find a job.

Guidelines to Building a Portfolio

To design an effective portfolio, you will need to do a little digging. Look to the past and ask yourself a few questions. What have I done? What skills have I mastered and practiced? What experiences do I have that have made me the quality person I am? What do I know? What have I done well? The point is to narrow the focus of your portfolio, and of course your career goals. Ask yourself the following questions:

- What paid employment have I had?

- What unpaid work have I done? This includes volunteering and any type of community service you might have done.

- What courses have I taken (particularly a category, such as animation classes or design classes) where I have gained skills and felt successful?

- What training have I had? This might include informal classes, seminars, groups of friends that gather with common interests (such as book groups), or specific programs?

- What skills do I have that make me capable of accomplishing tasks? Take some time with this question and really evaluate your skills. Listening, following directions, and other day-to-day tasks count as skills.

- Once you have answered these questions, you will then need to gather all of this information and organize it. It is at this point where you can start to see how one thing you have done is related to other things, or how one skill has built upon itself. Some items will be easy to display. You can photocopy a diploma or other award. An art collection can be photographed. A collage of photographs can be copied. For graphic design and animation, you can include printed items or storyboards.

After you have gathered everything you want to include, give it a second look. A portfolio should contain the best things about you as an artist not EVERYTHING about you. Decide which things are not important or not relevant to the goal.

For a specific position, you may want to include only 4 of 6 portions, for instance, if that is all that seems relevant to that job. Next, make a list of what your portfolio contains. You can use this as an attachment to your resume or cover letter. And always have a back-up portfolio in case something happens to your first one. You don't want to have to start completely over.

You will need a container for your portfolio. Something that looks nice and doesn't damage the items will work well. Accordion folders, small briefcase-type holders, or other similar carrying pockets can be used. Be sure to keep your portfolio updated and current.

The Electronic Portfolio

The same rules mentioned above apply to the electronic portfolio. Put your best items in and organize them neatly. The easiest way to create the electronic portfolio is to use an electronic format from the start. That is, documents and resumes could be placed on a Web page or disk as they are originated rather than trying to collect information and transfer it later to the electronic version later.

When you are ready to distribute the portfolio to potential employers, several options for making the portfolio information available exist. First, a number of employers, newspapers, and agencies have Web page postings. By going into these Web sites, directions can be followed as to how to post your own portfolio on the Web. Secondly, writing to employers with directions as to how to access your portfolio on your Web site can be included in your cover letter. Thirdly, the contents of the portfolio can be placed on a disk and distributed to potential employers.

The electronic portfolio presents many conveniences that the traditional portfolio lacks including the ability to reach many people and the demonstration of technology skills. But it's best to have both types of portfolios on hand.

Presentation of Your Portfolio

·   The portfolio contains only the best, professionally displayed examples of your work as an artist, assembled into a hand carried or electronic form. The items should simple, easy to see, easy to rearrange, and easy to understand.

·   The graphic design portfolio contains printed work. Illustrators will need printed and or original work and slide sets.

·   The media designer's portfolio is simply some combination of video tape, cd-rom, or floppy discs. Find a professional case that carries these materials well.

·   A fine artist's portfolio contains original work if two dimensional and not too large (prepared consistently). 35mm slides sets are a must for all types of work. 35mm slides, display transparencies, or color prints will be needed for large or three dimensional work. 35mm slides should be in pages. Color prints or display transparencies should be placed in vinyl or mylar pages and prepared consistently. Include significant articles or reviews, in protective pages, at the end of the portfolio.

- Take EVERY opportunity to examine the portfolios of working artists so that you can improve upon your own.

- Show your originality. Don't present yourself as being in the style of someone else.

- Be able to talk confidently about your work. Be ready to explain why you chose to do everything you did.

- Remember that this work is the past. Be confident, professional, at ease. Sell what you can do.

Organization of the Portfolio

- Place your "best" work first and last.

- Group work according to subject and content. Show a maximum of 10 to 15 pieces of work in design or illustration and only your best work.

- Illustrators: Focus on a style or media.

- Fine artists: The most recently completed body of work that shows a mature, conceptual investigation.

- Graphic Designers: Research interviews to see what will be appropriate to put in the portfolio.

Writing an Artist's Statement

"Art never expresses anything but itself. It has an independent life just as thought has, and develops purely on its own lines. It is not necessarily realistic in an age of realism, nor spiritual in an age of faith. So far from being the creation of its time, it is usually in direct opposition to it, and the only history that it preserves for us is the history of its own progress. Sometimes it returns upon its footsteps, and revives some antique form, as happened in the archaistic movement of late Greek art, and in the pre-Raphaelite movement of our own day. At other times it entirely anticipates its age, and produces in one century work that it takes another century to understand, to appreciate, and to enjoy."

–The Decay of Lying by Oscar Wilde

Your artist's statement should:

· Explain your personal involvement in art.

· Talk about the development of your style in terms of materials, process and composition. How do these things help you reach the goals of your work?

· What have been your influences? What artists, styles, movements or history do you identify with?

· What are the goals of your work?

· What are your goals as an artist?

· What do you want to communicate to your community?

You will probably have to write several drafts of your artist's statement until you feel like it is finally right. It takes time to articulate your purpose as an artist. You may not have even thought about it until you sat down to write you statement. But it will come to you and potential employers will be impressed that you are so focused. For job applications be clear and to the point. Your writing will need to be easily understood by a wide, general audience. Be practical and to the point, not arty. In an artist's statement, a conversational style is very effective. This statement is part of your portfolio, and might be used on a gallery wall or sent to publications as a press release. Be substantive but remain understandable to a wide audience.

The artist statement has one purpose: To express your creativity and integrity.

Writing Your Artist's Statement

You will need pencil and paper, a dictionary, and a thesaurus.

What Are You About?

1.   Take five minutes and think about why you do what you do. How did you get into this work? How do you feel when work is going well? What are your favorite things about your work? Jot down short phrases that capture your thoughts. Don't worry about making sense or connections.

2.   Make a list of words and phrases that communicate your feelings about your work and your values. Include words you like, words that make you feel good, words that communicate your values or fascinations. Be loose.

a. What do you like best about what you do?

b. What do you mean when you say that a piece has turned out really well?

c. What patterns emerge in your work? Is there a pattern in the way you select materials? In the way you use color, texture, or light?

d. What do you do differently from the way you were taught? Why?

3. Write five sentences that tell the truth about your connection to your work. If you are stuck, start by filling in the blanks below.

When I work with _____, I am reminded that _____.

When my work is going well, I am filled with a sense of _____.

When people see my work, I'd like them to _____.

Your First Draft

Write a three paragraph artist's statement. Keep your sentences authentic and direct. Use the present tense ("I am," not "I was," "I do," not "I did.") If this seems hard to do right away, try writing about an artist that you admire. What is it about them that you like and want to emulate in your own work? Then do your own artist's statement with the same care. Your artist's statement should be written in the first person. Refer to yourself with the pronouns "I, me, my." Use the format below.

First paragraph. Begin with a simple statement of why you do the work you do. Support that statement, telling the reader more about your goals and aspirations.

Second paragraph. Tell the reader how you make decisions in the course of your work. How and why do you select materials, techniques, themes? Keep it simple and tell the truth.

Third paragraph. Tell the reader a little more about your current work. How it grew out of prior work or life experiences. What are you exploring, attempting, challenging by doing this work.

Let it Sit

Your artist's statement is very personal. You won't get it right the first time, so don't expect to. After you have completed your first draft, let it sit overnight. Give yourself time to think about yourself as an artist. Think about what your mission is, what you want to contribute to the world with your work. This incubation period will also help you to polish your writing.

Read Your Statement Aloud

Reading your statement aloud will uncover some things that weren't clear before. Listen to the way your statement flows. Does it express the way you feel as an artist? Does it make a point? As you read your statement, some phrases will stick out, while others may seem drab and unimportant. Cut and rewrite if necessary. You may find that the truth is a simpler statement than the one you made. Keep reading and revising your statement until you hear music, the sound of your own beat. That's when you'll know that you're done. Once you're done, sign it, date it, make lots of copies and use it.

An Interview with Michael Klouda

Internet Design Manager for Toll Brothers, Inc.

After 14 years in the 3D computer graphics and animation industry, Michael Klouda changed his career direction to interactive media. For the past several years he has been helping build an award winning Internet development department at one of the nations leading builder of luxury homes. He handles all the hiring and internships so he sees a whole lot of resumes.

Employers often receive literally receive hundreds of responses to a job ad. How can applicants make sure their resume is read and portfolio viewed?

I look for a clean and professional looking resume. The people we are looking for are creative individuals and programmers and the resumes that we get are all over the place. My best advice is to organize them – do not "design" them even if you are creative. We may be looking for a creative individual, but a creative resume does not help – believe me. Your idea of creative will be someone else's idea of crap. Your resume will get at the very best 1 minute of review before it is either put in the trash or in a "yes" or "maybe" pile. We look at the tools you have used, the experience you have, your spelling and clarity of thought as you work on your resume. It is difficult to sum up all that you are one sheet of paper (1 sheet only please!), but you have to do it.

More companies are using decision support systems that administer questionnaires online or at a kiosk in the personnel office, combine the answers with a digital resume, and make a decision based on preset parameters. How do job applicants benefit from this system and how does an artist showcase samples of his/her creative portfolio in this environment?

I am not a big fan of this kind of tool for attracting employees in a creative environment. I do not think it is a fair way to judge a persons skills or personality. I would recommend an online portfolio for anyone in the creative field. If done well can really help you stand out. I can not tell you how many people have come looking for a job in our Web department that do not have any online examples!

Networking is about establishing informal relationships with other people, people who can provide information that can help in the job search. How does one find out about these networking meetings and how can applicants use networking to find the right job without being too pushy?

I do not like networking meetings myself because they do seem pushy and you need to act as a salesperson. Many people find this offensive or uncomfortable. Networking, however, is a very impor-tant task and needs to be done. I think the soft sell approach is the best. Have your business card handy and relax and be casual as you meet other people. Listen more than you talk and be prepared with something that you can give an important contact to look at later (samples or your resume or business card), The people you meet will be networking too and will usually be thinking about their needs a lot more than your needs. If they like you and have something to remember you by that can go a long way.

What are the benefits/drawbacks to including temp work or an internships on your resume?

Internships can give you some excellent experience at some good companies. I like them and we use a lot of interns. Sometimes interns do nothing that can further their career experience but can put a good company on the resume. If you're in a good place, you may actually get some great experience and work with some excellent people. This is what we try to do at my company. Sometimes you just need to get a job and make some money. If the temp job does not really fit in your career path you may want to leave it off you resume.

What are some of the advantages of applying to a small company versus a big company?

Often more personal contact with the people you would be working with happens in a small company. Sometimes smaller companies have more exciting projects going on and are more likely to let less experiences people in to work on them.

What are some of the things one should never say or do during a job interview?

Never curse — ever. Try to relax and be friendly. That shows confidence. Do not work at coming up with questions that you think they want to hear. Ask questions that you really need to know answers for.

Do job-seeking practices change for someone re-entering the job market?

Good questions. I do not know. They change slightly if you are changing careers, but I have found that the foundation of job searching remains the same. Be professional, quietly confident, and diligent and you will meet the right people to get you the right job.

What kinds of advantages do students finishing schools now have over those that entered the job market say ten years ago?

Well ten years ago the market was better than it is today, but our tools for finding jobs are also much greater. We expect a lot more out of our students these days as we assume that they have a lot of computer experience as opposed to ten years ago, so you may get less training but can also get a better position right out of school.

Michael Klouda
Internet Design Manager
Toll Brothers, Inc.
http://www.tollbrothers.com

Checking Your References

Few hiring managers trust their own judgment when making hiring decisions, especially at higher levels. That's why companies seek outside opinions. Pay attention to what others say, because nothing can hurt you worse than a lukewarm reference.

In seeking testimonials, don't limit yourself to former bosses. Anyone who knows your work can speak on your behalf. That includes peers, subordinates, suppliers, vendors, consultants, even customers. In short, those who've been above you, below you, and all around you.

Don't leave matters to chance, hoping your references will say the right thing. They may be taken off guard, or they may actually contradict you. The best way to proceed is to draft a statement for your reference person to sign or revise. Giving them the raw material simplifies their task. Remember, few busy managers like to write. It's time consuming, and they've often got urgent matters to handle. If you don't provide them with a written draft, your request for a reference letter may be delayed for weeks.

A well-written reference letter should address these issues:

1. Job title and dates of employment

2. Relationship of the writer

3. Key promotions

4. Duties and responsibilities

5. Work and/or management style

6. Areas of major strength

7. Specific results and achievements

As always, emphasize results and achievements. That's what sells.

International Companies

Working for an international company can be an exciting, challenging, and culturally enriching experience. But there are some key differences between working in a multinational firm and a local company—differences that can make a big impact on your job satisfaction, career path, and the relationships you make with your colleagues.

At a multinational firm, employees come from all over the world—bringing different languages, cultural traditions, and ethnic backgrounds with them. If you join an international company, your colleagues will probably speak English at some level, as well as the country's native language. Working in a multilingual environment is a great opportunity to meet a diverse group of people, gain international business experience, and improve your foreign language skills. Patience, understanding, and effective communication skills will help you establish stronger working relationships with foreign colleagues, and get the most out of your international experience.

Job seekers may also have more personal development opportunities at a multinational company than at a domestic firm. Many international companies have offices all over the world, and their employees may spend a year or two working abroad. If you are thinking about joining an international firm and are interested in working abroad, ask about potential employment exchange opportunities at the company's foreign offices.

Before applying to a multinational company, seek out friends, acquaintances, and other contacts that have experience in an international working environment. Ask about their day-to-day work schedule, their boss and coworkers, and the general culture and atmosphere of the firm before you decide whether working in an international environment might be the right choice for you.

Job Application Guidelines from Five Countries

If you are thinking about a job overseas, you may need to reformat your resume to fit the traditional requirements of the country where you'd like to work. Not only will it show potential employers that you've done your research, but it will also help you get acquainted with some of the customs of that particular country. Here are job application guidelines from five countries you may be interested in.

Canada

A job search in Canada starts with preparing a one-page letter. To get ideas for creating an electronic resume, check the Web site http://www.jobsearchcanada.com.

The resume includes the following:

- Contact information, centered at the top.

- Education, listing colleges and/or universities attended, dates of attendance, courses of study, and diplomas or degrees. In this section, you should also mention extra courses or training, internships, and foreign travel. List this information in reverse-chronological order.

· Work experience, giving the firm name, your title(s), dates of employment and responsibilities. State whether the work was temporary or part-time. If you have no job at the present, you should mention that fact also. Once again, the information should be listed in reverse-chronological order.

· Other skills, such as computer, and language fluency.

· Personal information, such as relevant volunteer activities and hobbies.

· Three references, with their titles and contact information.

In Canada, it is illegal for a prospective employer to ask your marital status, sexual orientation, race, or age, or to request a photo.

Japan

When applying for a position in Japan, you may submit a "rirekisho," a standard two-page form in Japanese with no cover letter, or a two-page American-style resume and cover letter in English.

If using the American-style resume, you should have your name and contact information centered at the top. The resume should begin with a summary of qualifications such as: nine years experience with IT, experience with international companies, strong Japanese-English bilingual skills.

Under "Employment Experience," list the names, locations, and focus of all former employers, with your dates of employment, title(s) and responsibilities. You need not list job accomplishments on the resume; you will discuss them at the interview.

Under "Education," list all schools you attended, dates of attendance, and diplomas or degrees. Add honors received, and special skills, such as fluency in specific computer applications, and standard language test scores.

End your resume with personal information: date of birth, marital status, and nationality. There are no enclosures necessary (except the cover letter) with the English resume; the "rirekisho" states that a photo should be attached.

Spain

When seeking a job in Spain, prepare a cover letter and resume. Copies of certificates, diplomas, and references will be required later. Type the cover letter, tailor it for the position, and mail it along with your resume and a small, quality photo.

If you have a short employment history, write your resume in chronological order to show your development. At the top of the resume, give personal information—name, place and date of birth, marital status, and home address and contact information.

In the "Education" section, list the institutions you attended with their locations, your academic emphases, diplomas, degrees, and dates of attendance. Also mention any honors received, levels of foreign language fluency, computer skills, and overseas travel or study. Include details about internships and part-time jobs.

For the "work experience" category, list the companies where you have been employed, their location and focus, your job title, responsibilities, achievements, and dates of employment. Remember to begin with your most recent work experience.

Complete your resume with a simple "References available upon request."

England

As part of your job application, you should include a one-page, tailored, cover letter. The letter should be business-like and addressed to a specific person.

Your resume may be two to three pages, depending on your experience. Start with your name, address, contact information, birth date, marital status, and nationality. If you are a non-EU citizen, clarify your work permit status. In what is called the "profile" section, give your professional designation (e.g., CPA), and immediate ambitions; then, in bullet-format, list relevant skills and a few work-related achievements.

Begin your employment history by describing your current position. Following the profile section, provide the name, location, and focus of each company, and your title and responsibilities. If you are new to the job market, you may include temporary or part-time positions.

The last major section is "education." In reverse-chronological order (most recent listed first) list schools attended, locations, areas of study, and diplomas/degrees. Mention additional courses and training, and special skills such as foreign language fluency and computer programs in which you are proficient.

At the end, it is sufficient to say: "References are available on request."

France

A job application in France should begin with a one page, handwritten cover letter (your handwriting may be used for character analysis). Include your resume with a photograph attached, but no other enclosures.

The resume itself should be relatively short, with a maximum of two pages. If you are a new job seeker, it may be even shorter. Begin with personal information: name, address, phone, and e-mail. Personal data, such as birth date, marital status, and children are optional.

Begin the section on education with your most recent study, and then list all schools attended, ending with your high (secondary) school. Give the name and location of each, your areas of study, degrees, and dates of attendance. Also, mention any additional courses, internships, or specialized training.

In the "Work Experience" section, list for each position the dates, the name, location, size, and type of company, and your title(s) and responsibilities. If you have many years of work experience, the education section follows your employment history.

At the end of the resume, you should list special competencies (such as level of expertise in foreign language, and computer skills), professional affiliations and volunteer experience, if relevant. State that references are "available on request."

For more information on conducting an international job search, go to http://www.goinglobal.com.

An Interview with Gary Quinn

Technical Manager at the University of Teesside in Canada

Gary Quinn performs hiring for the university and works with students on how to find employment.

Employers often receive literally receive hundreds of responses to a job ad. How can applicants make sure their resume is read and portfolio viewed?

Read the job description, responsibilities, personal specification, etc. Address all the points you can honestly. If you don't have experience of an "essential" say so. If you're willing to learn, then say so.

What are the benefits/drawbacks to including temp work or an internships on your resume?

You should include all your experience with dates. Otherwise you'll be asked to explain the gaps.

How can a recruiter help applicants that have little or no job experience, and what should their first step be?

Shouldn't the applicant take responsibility for their own experience and training? Lets think about this... If a recruiter has lots of applications, some with experience, some without... Who do they pick? The best a recruiter can do is offer advice when it's asked for.

What are the advantages to searching for a job online? What are some of the drawbacks?

Advantage: Search engines. Disadvantage: too many hits and inappropriate hits. I've seen job posts through recruitment agencies-and got the impression that none of the posts actually existed (unless specific companies and job details and salaries were listed). I came to the conclusion that the agencies were looking for CVs, rather than advertising specific jobs.

Should an applicant follow up the resume with a 'did you get it' phone call or what should their next step be after sending their resume?

If you've got it, you've had the phone call already. If not, most companies will give a reason why. But fear of legalities, etc will mean you get a diplomatic answer, and rarely the honest answer. Also remember that the person you speak to might just be a central point of contact, and not actually involved with the shortlisting or interviews, so might not know the real reasons. So forget it-get on with your life and the next application.

What are some of the advantages of applying to a small company versus a big company?

Small companies won't have a personnel department, so all the people on the interview panel will know what they're looking for, and will understand what you're talking about.

What are some of the things one should never say or do during a job interview?

Avoid negatives. Don't put yourself down in any way. If you have to say you can't do something or haven't done something follow up by saying you'll learn. Don't over sell, don't tell lies. Don't accept a coffee if you're going to spill it. Don't tell jokes, but funny experiences are ok if they're genuinely funny and don't make anyone look silly. Don't forget what you came for. Most companies are serious about filling the post. Are you serious about getting it?

Gary Quinn, VR Centre
Technical Manager
University of Teesside

SG Network Admin
Borough Road, Middlesbrough
Go Player
Cleveland, TS1 3BA

Gary@tees.ac.uk
+44 (0)1642 384303 fax 384310
http://vr.tees.ac.uk

Looking for a Job While You Still Have One

Since the best time to look for a job is when you are already employed, there are a set of tactics that you have got to use to do it successfully. If you are already employed, you have got be careful about posting your resume. Before posting to any of the large job sites, it's a good idea to peruse the listings first. You want to know if your current employer is using the database to post jobs. Because if they are, then chances are, they're also searching the resume databases, too. Very easily they could stumble upon yours. Be careful about answering blind ads; you don't know who's behind them.

And don't use your company email to send resumes or correspond with potential employers. Most companies now have "acceptable use policies" about company email and they may be scanning all incoming and outgoing mail. You don't want your boss reading your email about your job search.

Don't put your company email in your resume either. It's best to use your personal email while searching for a job online. You should also get an answering machine for your home phone and give out that number only. The same rules apply. You don't want your current employer to know that you're looking around until you're ready to tell them.

And while it may be tempting, you don't want to search for a job on company time. Not only will your employer find out, but also potential employers will figure out what you're doing and judge you negatively. Don't use any resources of your present employer, such as stationery, postage, telephone, fax machine, copy machine, computer, etc. It's just not good business.

Schedule interviews and make phone calls early in the morning, at lunchtime, during evenings and weekends. Use vacation time or personal days to interview. Potential employers will judge you better than if you "called in sick". If you do it to your current employer you'll do it to a new employer as well. If you need to use references from your current employer, select people who have left the company or those employees that will understand the importance of confidentiality.

It may take longer to find a new job while you still have one, but doing it right can make the difference between you finding a better position or being in a rose one. Using some of the tools that the Internet has brought forth can not only speed up your job search, but assist you in keeping it confidential as well. Remember to be courteous to both your current and future employers.

An Interview with Barbara Wolford

General Manager Graphic Arts Employment Specialists, Inc.

Employers often receive literally receive hundreds of responses to a job ad. How can applicants make sure their resume is read and portfolio viewed?

They need to specify a job objective and be simple about it. If it is a programmer for a certain process, then state that. Not something like a long, generic sentence.

Networking is about establishing informal relationships with other people, people who can provide information that can help in the job search. How does one find out about these networking meetings and how can applicants use networking to find the right job without being too pushy?

There are many resources online. Something as simple as monster.com can point you to your industry and ways to communicate with that group. One great one that might be specific for your organization is communication arts at http://www.commarts.com.

What are the benefits/drawbacks to including temp work or an internships on your resume?

Positive: it shows experience, it shows willingness to work in the industry at a young age instead of a job at taco bell. Another positive thing is in an office environment, the intern sees the relationship and hierarchy of personnel. Learns the players and is better adjusted to an office environment if that is the route they choose. If in animation, they learn who the head creative, sees the decision process, etc. Negative: it is usually the grunt work. Copying, faxing, answering phones and not much else experience.

How can a recruiter help applicants that have little or no job experience, and what should their first step be?

A resume. We spend many hours critiquing resumes when we have time. Giving advice, etc. to young people. Some are so clueless we sometimes do not have the patience. But if an individual shows the interest and the desire to get ahead, we will help.

Should an applicant follow up the resume with a 'did you get it' phone call or what should their next step be after sending their resume?

Wait for a response. If no response in a week, contact them.

What are some of the advantages of applying to a small company versus a big company?

You have a job where you wear more hats.

What are some of the things one should never say or do during a job interview?

Never bad-mouth your current situation. The employer will wonder what negative things you would say about them after you leave.

Do job-seeking practices change for someone re-entering the job market?

Yes, there needs to be an explanation of where you were and what you were doing. If reentering the job market, state took time off and why.

Barbara Wolford, General Manager
Graphic Arts Employment Specialists, Inc.

Glossary of Job-Seeking Terms

A

Accomplishments: The achievements you have had in your career. These key points really help sell you to an employer and they are much more than everyday job duties or responsibilities. When writing your cover letter and resume, be sure to highlight key accomplishments, big or small.

Action Verbs: The building blocks of effective cover letters and resumes. These concrete, descriptive verbs express your skills, assets, experience, and accomplishments. Begin each descriptive section with an action verb.

Assessment: These tests ask you a series of questions and try to provide you with some sense of your personality and career interests. The results can be a good starting point for discovering more about yourself and your interests and deciding which area of the arts you may fit best in.

B

Benefits: An important part of your compensation package, and part of the salary negotiation process. Every employer offers a different mix of benefits. These benefits may include paid vacations, company holidays, personal days, sick leave, life insurance, medical insurance, retirement and pension plans, tuition assistance, child care, stock options, and more.

C

Career Change: Changing your occupation by devising a strategy to find new career choices. You may decide on a career change because you don't enjoy the work as much as you used to or because can't progress further in your career.

Career Fair: Career fairs offer a chance for a company to meet and screen a large volume of potential job candidates while simultaneously an opportunity for job seekers to meet and screen a large number of employers. These are often held at colleges or large corporations.

Career Objective/Job Objective: An optional part of your resume, but something you should consider including. It can sharpen the focus of your resume and should be as specific as possible explaining how you the candidate can benefit the employer.

Career Planning: The continuous process of evaluating your current lifestyle, likes/dislikes, passions, skills, personality, dream job, and current job and career path and making corrections and improvements to better prepare for future steps in your career.

Case Interview: See Job Interviewing.

Chronological Resume: See Resume.

Cold Call — When a job-seeker approaches an employer who has not publicly announced any job openings.

Compensation Package: The combination of salary and fringe benefits an employer provides to an employee. When evaluating a job offer, you should consider the whole package, not just salary.

Contract Employee: Also called a freelance employee, this is where you work for one organization that sells your services to another company on a project or time basis.

Corporate Culture: The collection of beliefs, expectations, and values shared by an organization's members and transmitted from one generation of employees to another.

Counter Offer/Counter Proposal: A salary negotiation technique used by job seekers when a job offer is not at an acceptable level. Most elements of a job offer are negotiable including the salary.

Cover Letter: A cover letter should always accompany your resume unless stated otherwise. A good cover letter opens a window to your personality and describes specific strengths and skills you offer the employer.

Curriculum Vitae: See Resume.

D

Declining Letter: A letter sent to an employer to turn down a job offer. When writing a declining letter, be sure to keep the door open. Be gracious and turn down the offer diplomatically.

Degrees & Certifications: Recognition bestowed on students upon completion of a unified program of study, including high school, trade schools, colleges and universities, and other agencies.

Domino Effect: States that five key phases comprise any good job search, and if you ignore any one of them or conduct one poorly, the likelihood of a successful job search decreases dramatically. Just as if you pulled a domino out of a row of dominos.

Dress for Success: First coined by author John Malloy in the 1970s, the term Dress for Success signifies tailoring one's attire, grooming, and overall appearance toward making a great first impression in a job interview, as well as maintaining a professional look while on the job to aid career advancement.

E

Email Cover Letter: A cover letter that is sent to the employer electronically via email.

F

Freelancer/Consultant/Independent Contractor: Where you work for yourself and bid for temporary jobs and projects with one or more employers.

Functional Resume: See Resume.

H

Hidden Job Market: Only about 5-20 percent of all job openings are ever publicly known, which results in about four-fifths of the job market being "closed." Strategies for

- Phone. These interviews have only one purpose: to decide if there is a good enough match to justify a site visit. Make sure to set a specific time for your telephone interview so you can be prepared.

Job Offer: See Offer of Employment.

Job Shadowing: One of the most popular work-based learning activities because it provides job seekers with opportunities to gather information on a wide variety of career possibilities before deciding where they want to focus their attention. Job shadows involve brief visits to a variety of workplaces, during which time you "shadow," observe, and ask questions of individual workers.

Job Skills: The skills you need to do a particular job.

Job Skills Portfolio: A job-seeking tool that you develop to give employers a complete picture of who you are, including samples of your work, your experience, your education, your accomplishments, your skill sets, and what you have the potential to become. A Job Skills Portfolio includes much more than a resume and cover letter.

K

Key Accomplishments: This is an optional part of a resume but one that is growing in popularity. This section should summarize your major career accomplishments.

Keywords: Nouns and noun phrases that relate to the skills and experience that employers use to recall resumes scanned into a database. Keywords can be precise "hard" skills — job-specific/professionspecific/industry-specific skills, technological terms and descriptions of technical expertise, job titles, certifications, names of products and services, industry buzzwords, etc.

L

Letter of Acceptance: A letter used to confirm the offer of employment and the conditions of the offer; i.e., salary, benefits, starting employment date, etc. It is always a good idea to get the entire offer in writing.

Letter of Agreement: A brief letter outlining the conditions of employment. Whether initiated by the employer or the candidate, it is always a good idea to get your entire offer in writing.

Letter of Interest: See Cover Letter.

Letter of Recommendation: A letter of support for your skills, ability, and work ethic, usually written by a former boss or co-worker, but could also be from a teacher or personal reference.

M

Mentor: A person at a higher level within a company or within your profession who counsels you and helps guide your career. A mentor relationship is one where the outcome of the relationship is expected to benefit all parties in the relationship for personal growth, career development, lifestyle enhancement, spiritual fulfillment, goal achievement, and other areas mutually designated by the mentor and partner.

N

Networking: Means of developing a broad list of contacts and encouraging them assist you in looking for a job. People in your network may be able to give you job leads, offer you advice and information about a particular company or industry, and introduce you to others so that you can expand your network.

O

Occupational Outlook Handbook: Published by the U.S. Department of Labor, Bureau of Labor Statistics, this guide provides detailed information on more than 250 occupations. The Handbook discusses the nature of the work and the typical working conditions for persons in each occupation. In addition, it details the requirements for entry and the opportunities for advancement.

Offer of Employment: An offer by an employer to a prospective employee that usually specifies the terms of an employment arrangement, including starting date, salary, benefits, working conditions. Also called a job offer.

R

Recruiters/Headhunters/Executive Search Firms: Professionals who are paid by employers to find candidates for specific positions. They often recruit candidates, but job seekers can also approach them.

References: A group of people who will say good things about you and who know specifics strengths that you offer. Can include work references, educational references, and personal references. These are never included on a resume, but are submitted only upon request.

Researching Companies: The process of gathering information about a company, its products, its locations, its corporate culture, and its financial successes. This information is extremely valuable in a job interview where you can show off your knowledge of the company, and can also help you in writing your cover letter.

Resume: A key job-seeking tool used to get an interview, it summarizes your accomplishments, your education, as well as your work experience, and should reflect your special mix of skills and strengths. There are several types of resumes:

· Chronological resumes are organized by your employment history in reverse chronological order, with company/job titles/accomplishments/dates of employment.

· Functional resumes are organized by skills and functions; bare-bones employment history often listed as a separate section.

· Text/scannable resumes are resumes that have been prepared to maximize the job seeker's visibility in an electronic resume database or electronic resume tracking system.

· Web-based resumes reside on the Web. A Web-based resume can range from quite ordinary to very elaborate. Fundamental principles of good resume writing, content, and design apply.

- Curriculum Vitae (CV) is similar to a resume, but more formal, and includes a detailed listing of items beyond the typical resume items, such as publications, presentations, professional activities, honors, and additional information.

S

Salary: The financial compensation an employee receives for performing a job. It can be determined by hourly, daily, weekly, monthly, and yearly. It also includes overtime pay, bonuses, and commissions.

Salary History: Some employers will request that you submit a salary history. A salary history tells them the level and frequency of your promotions.

Salary Negotiation: An extremely important process in which job seekers attempt to obtain the best compensation package possible, based on skills and experience, the industry salary range, and the company's guidelines.

Salary Requirements: Some employers may ask you to state the salary you require for a specific job opening. If your salary requirement is too high, you won't get an offer. If it's too low, you won't get what you're worth. The best strategy is to state that you're open to any fair offer and are willing to negotiate.

Scannable Resume: See Resume.

T

Temporary (Temp) Agency/Staffing Firm: Companies that place workers in jobs on a contract or temporary basis.

Testing: You may be asked to take a variety of tests during your job search, from aptitude and personality tests to honesty and drug tests.

Thank You Letters: You should send a letter thanking each person who has interviewed you. It's just common courtesy and it will make you stand out from the crowd.

Transferable Skills: Skills you have acquired during any activity in your life. This includes jobs, classes, projects, parenting, hobbies, and sports.

V

Vita: See Resume.

W

Workplace Values: Concepts and ideas that define a job-seeker and influence your satisfaction. Not only in the workplace, but with life in general. Job seekers should perform a values check every few years to make sure their career is on track.

Professional Organizations

American Advertising Federation, http://www.aaf.org/

The American Advertising Federation protects and promotes the well-being of advertising. They accomplish this through a unique, nationally coordinated grassroots network of advertisers, agencies, media companies, local advertising clubs and college chapters.

American Arts Alliance, http://www.artswire.org/~aaa/

The American Arts Alliance is a principal advocate for professional non-profit arts organizations.

American Institute of Graphic Artists, http://www.aiga.org/

The purpose of AIGA is to further excellence in communication design as a broadly defined discipline, strategic tool for business and cultural force. AIGA is the place design professionals turn to first to exchange ideas and information, participate in critical analysis and research and advance education and ethical practice.

American Marketing Association, http://www.marketingpower.com/

The American Marketing Association is here to help you, the marketer. With focused information and insights, AMA is the resource to use every day for help with business challenges, professional development, and your career.

American Society of Association Executives, http://www.asaenet.org/

ASAE, known as the association of associations, is considered the advocate for the non-profit sector. The society is dedicated to advancing the value of voluntary associations to society and supporting the professionalism of the individuals who lead them.

Art Directors Club, http://www.adcny.org/

Based in New York, this is an international not for profit organization of leading creatives in advertising, graphic design, interactive media, broadcast design, typography, environmental design, photography, illustration, and related disciplines. Job listings are included on this site.

ArtsEdNet, http://www.artsednet.getty.edu/

Provides information on curriculum ideas and links to several other Web sites for art education, including publications.

Association for Women in Communications, http://www.womcom.org/

The Association for Women in Communications is a professional organization that champions the advancement of women across all communications disciplines by recognizing excellence, promoting leadership and positioning its members at the forefront of the evolving communications era.

American Institute of Graphic Artists (AIGA)
http://www.aiga.com

For the graphic arts professional in design, illustration and photography. This is the oldest and most important organization in the field. This is a key organization for professional workshops, publications, and contacts/networking.

American Society of Media Photographers (ASMP)
http://www.asmp.org

This a leading and highly active professional organization. This is a key organization for professional workshops, publications, and contacts.

National Art Education Association (NAEA)
http://www.naea.org

As the name explains, the professional association for art teachers. Membership in WAEA includes membership in NAEA.

National Arts Support

Foundation Center
79 Fifth Avenue
New York, NY 10003
(212) 620-4230

Visual Arts Program National Endowment for the Arts
1100 Pennsylvania Avenue NW
Washington, DC 20506
(202) 682-5448

Arts Organizations

American Council for the Arts
1 East 53rd St., 7th Floor
New York, NY 10022
(212) 223-2728

American Craft Council
72 Spring Street
New York, NY 10012
(212) 274-0630

American Institute of Graphic Arts (AIGA)
164 Fifth Ave.
New York, NY 10010
(212) 807-1990

American Society of Media Photographers (ASMP)
14 Washington Road, Suite 502
Princeton Junction, NJ 08550
(609) 799-8300

Arts, Crafts, and Theater Safety
181 Thompson St., #23
New York, NY 10012
(212) 777-0062

The Comic Book Professionals Association
P. O. Box 570850
Tarzana, CA 91357

Center for Safety in the Arts
5 Beekman St., Suite 820
New York, NY 10023
(212) 787-6557

College Art Association
275 Seventh Ave., 5th Floor
New York, NY 10001
(212) 691-1051

Graphic Artists Guild
11 West 20th St., 8th Floor
New York, NY 10011
(212) 463-7730

International Sculpture Center
1050 17th St. NW, Suite 250
Washington, DC 20036
(202) 785-1144

Metropolitan Regional Arts Council (MRAC)
2423 University Ave. West, Suite 114
Saint Paul, MN 55114 (612) 645-0402

Midwest Media Artists Access Center
2388 University Ave.
Saint Paul, MN 55114
(612) 644-1912

Motion Picture Screen Cartoonists Union
Local 839 IATSE

4729 Lankershim Boulevard
North Hollywood, CA 91602
(818) 766-7151

National Art Education Association
1916 Association Drive
Reston, VA 22091

National Artists Equity Association
1325 G St. NW
Washington, DC 20006
(202) 628-9633

National Association of Schools of Art and Design
11250 Roger Bacon Drive, Suite 21
Reston, VA 22090
(703) 437-0700

Job Search Journal

Personal Contact Data

Name

Address

City/State/Zip

Phone

Facsimile

Mobile

E-mail

Home Page
http://

Place of birth

Date of birth

List the short-term goals you want to accomplish. Examples might include completion of specific classes or networking with other professionals. Enter a date before you begin writing so you know when you made your entries.

Short-term Career Goals

Intermediate goals might include completion of a certificate or degree program, taking and passing your certification exams, or getting a certain amount of paid work experience under your belt before making your next career move.

Intermediate Career Goals

Your long-term goals are somewhat dependent on where you are in your career and what you want to accomplish. A long-term goal, may mean being in an executive position. For others, it may mean completing a script or other creative project. If you don't have any long-term career goals, it's time to find some.

Long-term Career Goals

Where would you like to see your education go? Here, add any work-related training that would be beneficial for your career.

Education and/or Training Goals

_____

_____

What are your personality traits or characteristics you are especially proud of or good at? List them here. You can also list the skills you possess that you consider to be your strengths.

Personal Strengths

_____

_____

Personal Weaknesses

_____

_____

If you have your own home page or online resume, list it here.

Home page or URL for your online resume, if any

http://_____

List any friends or colleagues you feel comfortable calling on for career advice or help with a future job search effort.

Career Networking Contacts

_____

_____

_____

_____

References generally fit into three categories: Personal references, Business or professional references, and character references. Of course, business references are the most common, but don't overlook providing other types of references, including personal ones. And remember to always let the person know you are putting them down as a reference so they're not caught off guard.

References

Personal

_____

_____

_____

Business

_____

_____

_____

Character

_____

_____

_____

List your formal education and degrees earned in this section.

Education

_____

_____

Here's the place to list any vocational, on-the-job or self-acquired (e.g. CBT) training you may have completed.

Training

_____

_____

If you hold any professional or vendor-specific certifications or occupational licenses, list them here. Be sure to include the effective date and if lapsed or still active.

Professional Certifications, Industry Certifications or Occupational Licenses

_____

_____

You'll want to keep track of any significant volunteer work or unpaid work experience here. This can be especially important for re-entry job seekers or others who may be able to use the information to their advantage at some future date or when making a career change.

Unpaid or Volunteer Experience

_____

_____

_____

_____

This is the obvious one. List the part and full-time jobs you've held here, whether or not they relate to your current career. You never know if or when you'll end up making a career change. Include the position(s) you held, employer name and dates of employment as a minimum. Remember that if is often helpful to describe your "functional" job duties or responsibilities, rather than what is implied by the job title.

Paid Work Experience

_____

_____

_____

_____

If you have any articles or documents you authored, co-authored and published, list them here. You will want to list the title, copyright and/or publication date, as well as the publisher.

Articles & Publications

_____

_____

_____

_____

You may not have any personal contacts with recruiters, executive search firms or headhunters, but if you do, or if you meet someone in that line of work, jot down their contact info for future reference.

Recruiting Contacts

_____

_____

_____

_____

Whenever you've completed a project or assignment of any significance, or feel you accomplished something of value, write it down here. You never know when the information can be put to future use. Also, it's good to see your accomplishments written down. It's a good remeinder of where you've been and where you're going. Update this section every 6 months or so.

Completed Projects & Accomplishments